MASTERCHEF
1991

FOREWORD BY LOYD GROSSMAN

GENERAL EDITOR: JANET ILLSLEY

EBURY PRESS
LONDON

First Published 1991 by Ebury Press
an imprint of the Random Century Group
Random Century House
20 Vauxhall Bridge Road
London   SW1V 2SA

Second Impression 1991

MasterChef 1991
A Union Pictures production for BBC TV Elstree
Series devised by Franc Roddam
Executive Producer: Bradley Adams
Producer and Director: Richard Bryan
Production Manager: Joy Spink
Production Co-ordinator: Helen Gurry

General Editor: Janet Illsley
Production, Design & Setting: Clive Dorman
Front Cover Photograph: Helen Pask
Back Cover Photograph: Richard Farley
Food Photography: Jerry Tubby
Home Economist: Meg Jansz

A catalogue record for this book is available from
the British Library

ISBN 0 09 175215 9

Printed and bound in Great Britain by
Butler & Tanner Ltd., Frome and London

CONTENTS

FOREWORD

The first Earl of Lytton is remembered by historians, if at all, for his four year stint as Viceroy of India, but Lytton preferred fame as a poet writing under the pen name of Owen Meredith. Most of what he wrote is now forgotten, but food lovers are probably familiar with a few of his lines:

We may live without poetry, music and art;
We may live without conscience and live without heart;
We may live without friends; we may live without books;
But civilised man cannot live without cooks.

Overstating the case, but certainly making the point that good cooking, like good friends, good books and a good conscience is an indispensable part of civilised life. After two series of *MasterChef* I can say with great confidence that when measured by the cooks' rule of thumb, ie more cooks equal more civilisation, the state of British civilisation in 1991 is very good indeed.

The 1990 series proved that "the British Grand Prix for amateur chefs" was not only a good idea of Franc Roddam's but a good idea that was fun and encouraged a lot of first rate cooks to come forward. The 1991 series showed that there are a lot of *great* cooks in this country. Throughout the first year's competition the judges and I were almost pinching ourselves because it was all so much better than we had any reasonable right to expect from amateurs. This time the judges' most frequent words were once again "I'd be happy to pay for that in a restaurant". This year, however, it was coupled with some speculation that the word amateur was losing its meaning if amateurs could produce such great food. One of our most famous chefs hauled me aside for a word and enquired "are you *sure* she's not a professional?" Indeed she was not.

Based on this year's cooking it's fair to observe that our long night of slavish devotion to French cooking is now over. The traditional British love of puddings and, I'm thrilled to say, potatoes was in evidence. Indian, Middle Eastern, Italian and American influences were a delicious testimony to our broadening national palate. Few of our contestants, both in the regional "cookoffs" and the televised competitions, were cooking to show off. Instead they were cooking to delight. Pointless elaboration and novelty were decidedly out and freshness and flavour were very much in.

And what flavours we were lucky enough to taste this year. Flavours like the eastern spice of cardamom and the earthy tang of wild mushrooms. And plenty of humble but utterly fabulous ingredients like wild pigeon and mussels. A few trends surprised me. Fruit turned up in pretty unlikely places and the trend towards more "raw food" and salads is gathering pace rather more quickly than I would have predicted.

A lot of the food we ate could I suppose be called "high class peasant food": that is, food which was honest, sturdy and unpretentious. Food that *dared* to be simple. A constant theme that emerged from my chats with the judges was keeping it simple. The great French food journalist Curnonsky wrote that 'In cooking as in all the arts, simplicity is the sign of perfection.' The age of food in fancy dress is , thank God, finished. Simple perfection is replacing the idea that cooking is either a branch of interior decoration or one of the higher sciences.

Throughout all the publicity and press during the series the two questions that I was asked most frequently were "Was it really that good?" and "Were there any disasters?" "Yes" it really was that good and "no" there were no disasters; an absolute tribute to the talent of our contestants and the professionalism, care and unceasing good humour of our production team and technical crew. Brad Adams, our executive producer, and Richard Bryan, our producer and director, were hugely helpful to me and more importantly to the contestants.

Judging was a struggle this year and I had to repeatedly point out to our competitors that they all deserved to win and that they were all on the programme because they were already winners. It was a pleasure to meet them and my greatest regret was that they all couldn't be *MasterChef of Britain 1991.*

Our judges often remarked that cooking was a matter of passion and love and sharing. You might say that one ought to cook from the heart first, the stomach second and the head last. Our competitors cooked with great heart from the very beginning and I shall always be grateful to all of them.

Loyd Grossman

Notes for Recipe Users

Quantities are given in metric and imperial measures.
Follow one set of measurements only, not a
combination, because they are not interchangeable.
All spoon measures are level.
Fresh herbs are used unless otherwise stated.

INTRODUCTION

The recipes featured in this book are those of the twenty seven people who were selected to represent their regions in the televised competition. However, there was an enormous demand to enter *MasterChef 1991,* and we thought that readers might be interested to learn how the successful applicants were selected, and some of the rules of the competition.

On the basis of their completed forms, careful scrutiny of their recipes, and telephone conversations, sixteen were selected from each of nine regions based around major cities. These successful contestants were invited to a regional "cook-off" at the city catering college were I was joined by the chef from a respected local restaurant and a lecturer from the college to taste sixteen wonderful meals. With great difficulty, and much "deliberation and cogitation", we eventually selected our three winners from each region.

Our twenty seven finalists each cooked for Loyd Grossman and his guests in front of six television cameras in a London studio. They had $2^1/2$ hours to prepare a three-course meal for four people, and their maximum budget was thirty pounds. Once the cooking had started, whatever happened happened - there were no retakes! And each week more than five million people have watched.

At the end of each show the crew, who had watched and savoured the meals throughout the cooking, fell upon the uneaten portions. We hope that you get as much pleasure from preparing and enjoying the menus in this book as they, and their creators, have given us.

RICHARD BRYAN
Producer and Director
MasterChef

REGIONAL HEATS

THE SOUTH EAST

JENNIFER TWYDELL • ASHLEY DAVIES • MELANIE JAPPY

WINNER

JENNIFER TWYDELL

Jennifer was brought up in the Middle East and only returned to Britain five years ago from Quatar. She now lives with husband Richard and her two young children in Guildford, in a house filled with batik, brass figurines and other artifacts.

Now in her fourth year of an Open University science and technology degree, Jennifer is also a keen bird watcher, spending many an afternoon in the local hide. At home she relaxes with her piano and embroidery.

JENNIFER TWYDELL'S MENU

STARTER

Mussels in a Creamy Curry Sauce

"MUSSELS AND CURRY — VERY GOOD COMBINATION"
ALASTAIR LITTLE

MAIN COURSE

Spiced Loin of Lamb 'Khouzi'
Nut Pilaf
Imam Bayildi (Stuffed Aubergines)
Fattoush (Toasted Bread Salad)

DESSERT

Baked Fruit in Foil

"OH JENNIFER — THIS IS TERRIFIC"   CHARLES DANCE

MUSSELS IN A CREAMY CURRY SAUCE

1.4kg (3 lb) live mussels, scrubbed
90ml (3 fl oz) dry white wine
1 small onion, chopped
1 clove garlic, chopped
thyme sprig
parsley sprig
freshly ground black pepper

Curry Sauce:
25g (1 oz) butter
15g (1/2 oz) plain flour
1 clove garlic, chopped
5ml (1 tsp) curry paste
salt and freshly ground pepper
1 egg yolk
squeeze of lemon juice
1/4 pint (5 fl oz) double

Garnish:
chopped parsley

Put the mussels in a pan with the wine, onion, garlic, herbs and pepper. Cover and cook over high heat, shaking the pan frequently, until the mussels have just opened; discard any unopened ones. Remove the mussels and strain the liquor through a muslin-lined sieve; keep on one side. Discard the empty half shells and keep the mussels warm in their serving dishes.

To make the sauce, melt the butter in a pan, stir in the flour and cook, stirring, until golden. Add the garlic, curry paste and strained liquor and stir well until smooth. Season to taste with salt and pepper. Simmer, stirring, for 5 minutes. In a bowl, mix the egg yolk with the lemon juice and cream. Slowly pour in the hot sauce, stirring.

Pour the curry sauce over the mussels and garnish with chopped parsley to serve.

SPICED LOIN OF LAMB "KHOUZI"

This recipe is based on the Middle Eastern dish "Khouzi" in which a roast lamb is stuffed with chickens and laid on a bed of rice mixed with nuts, onions and fruit, lavishly garnished with egg, tomatoes, olives etc.

700g (1 1/2 lb) boned loin of lamb
2 cloves garlic, sliced
15ml (1 tbsp) olive oil
15ml (1 tbsp) lemon juice
10ml (2 tsp) baharat spice (see below)
salt
a little lamb stock (optional)

Trim as much fat from the meat as possible. Tie into a neat cylindrical shape. Insert slivers of garlic along the length of meat. Pour the oil and lemon juice over the meat and rub well in. Sprinkle with baharat spice and season with salt. Leave to marinate for at least 1 hour.

Roast in a preheated oven at 180°C (350°F) mark 4 for about 30 minutes, until cooked but still pink inside, basting frequently with the pan juices. Add a little lamb stock to the pan if necessary, to prevent the juices burning. Leave the meat to rest for 10 minutes before slicing and arranging on the nut pilaf. Spoon the pan juices over the meat to serve.

BAHARAT SPICE

Grind 60ml (4 tbsp) black peppercorns, 45ml (3 tbsp) cumin seeds, 30ml (2 tbsp) each coriander seeds, cassia bark and cloves, with 5ml (1 tsp) cardamom seeds in a grinder or blender. Mix with 2 grated whole nutmegs and 60ml (4 tbsp) paprika. Store in an airtight jar.

NUT PILAF

125g (4 oz) basmati rice
few saffron strands
1 loomi (dried lime)
900ml (1½ pints) water
10ml (2 tsp) salt
5cm (2 inch) piece of cassia bark

Nut Mixture:
15ml (1 tbsp) olive oil
1 large onion, quartered and sliced
5ml (1 tsp) sugar
25g (1 oz) flaked almonds
25g (1 oz) pine nuts
50g (2 oz) cashew nuts
50g (2 oz) sultanas
salt and freshly ground pepper

Garnish:
tomatoes, olives, hard-boiled egg wedges,
lemon wedges, parsley or coriander sprigs

Wash the rice thoroughly until the water runs clear. Soak the saffron strands in a little boiling water for 10 minutes. Pierce the loomi with a sharp knife or skewer in several places. Put the rice in a pan with the water, salt, cassia, loomi and saffron. Bring to the boil and cook for 10 minutes or until just tender.

Meanwhile, prepare the nut mixture. Heat the olive oil in a pan, add the onion and sugar and fry until golden brown. Add the nuts and continue to fry until the onions and nuts are nicely browned. Add the sultanas and season with salt and pepper.

Drain the rice, discarding the loomi and cassia. Toss with the nut mixture and transfer to warmed serving plates. Add the spiced lamb and garnish the finished dish with any or all of the suggested garnish ingredients as desired!

IMAM BAYILDI (STUFFED AUBERGINES)

2 medium aubergines
30ml (2 tbsp) olive oil
1 large onion, sliced
1 clove garlic, chopped
230g (8 oz) can chopped tomatoes
15ml (1 tbsp) chopped coriander
15ml (1 tbsp) chopped parsley
5ml (1 tsp) ground cumin
salt and freshly ground pepper
squeeze of lemon juice
5ml (1 tsp) sugar
coriander sprigs to garnish

Remove stems from the aubergines. Peel off 1cm (½ inch) strips of skin lengthwise to give a striped effect. Split the aubergines in half lengthwise and cut a deep slit along the flesh of each half, stopping short of the top and base, and ensuring you do not cut through the bottom. Salt the aubergines and leave to drain for 30 minutes. Rinse and dry thoroughly.

Heat 15ml (1 tbsp) olive oil in a frying pan and quickly brown the aubergines. Remove from the pan. Add the remaining oil to the pan and cook the onion and garlic until soft; do not brown. Add the tomatoes and simmer until the sauce has thickened slightly. Remove from the heat and add the herbs, cumin, salt and pepper, lemon juice and sugar. Cool slightly, then stuff the aubergines with this mixture, piling it on top.

Place the stuffed aubergines, side by side in an ovenproof dish, adding 1-2 tablespoons water to the dish. Bake in a preheated oven at 180°C (350°F) mark 4 for 30-40 minutes. Garnish with coriander to serve.

FATTOUSH (TOASTED BREAD SALAD)

1 pitta bread, toasted
few crisp lettuce leaves, shredded
1/2 cucumber, peeled and chopped
2 tomatoes, chopped
1 green pepper, chopped
6 spring onions, chopped
60ml (4 tbsp) chopped parsley
30ml (2 tbsp) chopped mint

Dressing:
60ml (4 tbsp) olive oil
60ml (4 tbsp) lemon juice
1 clove garlic, crushed
salt and freshly ground black pepper

Cut the pitta bread into small squares. Place in a salad bowl with the rest of the salad ingredients and mix lightly. Combine the ingredients for the dressing in a screw-topped jar and shake well. Pour over the salad and toss just before serving.

BAKED FRUIT IN FOIL

This recipe is based on Anton Mosimann's Baked Bananas.

1 orange
6 passion fruit, halved
2 bananas, halved lengthwise
1 small pineapple, peeled, cored and sliced
12 strawberries
60ml (4 tbsp) Cointreau
squeeze of lemon juice
1 vanilla pod, cut into 4 pieces
icing sugar for sprinkling
4 mint sprigs to decorate

Peel and segment the orange, discarding all pith. Scoop out the seeds and pulp from the passion fruit and purée in a blender or food processor, then sieve to remove pips.

Cut 4 even-sized rectangles of foil. Divide the fruit equally between them. Sprinkle with Cointreau and lemon juice. Pop in a piece of vanilla pod. Seal the pockets and bake in a preheated oven at 200°C (400°F) mark 6 for about 10 minutes.

Open the foil packets just before serving, adding a sprig of mint and a sprinkling of icing sugar.

REGIONAL HEATS
THE SOUTH EAST

JENNIFER TWYDELL • ASHLEY DAVIES • MELANIE JAPPY

ASHLEY DAVIES

A project manager for the Civil Aviation Authority, Ashley lives in a beautiful Georgian house in historic and peaceful Ramsgate. It is built upon intriguing Flemish cellars which Ashley keeps well stocked with carefully chosen wines.

All keen musicians, the Davies family trio — Ashley on keyboards, his wife Jan on Flute and son Owen on the trombone — keep their spirits up with regular jam sessions before Ashley slips down to the George and Dragon for a well-earned pint and to captain his team in the Thanet league pub quiz.

ASHLEY DAVIES' MENU

STARTER
Trout and Cheese Tartlets

"A QUICHE THAT EVEN A REAL MAN CAN EAT"   LOYD

"I LOVE LITTLE TARTLETS — THERE'S SOMETHING OLD FASHIONED ABOUT THEM"   ALASTAIR LITTLE

MAIN COURSE
Lamb in a Sweet Herb Crust
Gratin Dauphinois
Crunchy Carrot Purée
Stir-fried Mangetout

DESSERT
Peaches Poached with Lemon and Brandy

TROUT AND CHEESE TARTLETS

Avoid over-filling the pastry cases otherwise the mixture is likely to overflow as it rises slightly during cooking - causing the tartlets to stick to the tins.

Pastry:
125g (4 oz) plain flour
75g (3 oz) butter
1 egg yolk
15ml (1 tbsp) lemon juice
25g (1 oz) Parmesan cheese, freshly grated
salt and freshly ground pepper

Filling:
1 medium trout
2 spring onions, finely chopped
75g (3 oz) cottage cheese, drained
1 egg, beaten
60ml (4 tbsp) single cream
75g (3 oz) shelled prawns
freshly ground pepper

To make the pastry, sift the flour into a bowl and rub in the butter until sand-like in texture. In a cup, mix the egg yolk, lemon juice, cheese and salt and pepper. Pour over the flour mixture and mix to a soft dough. Chill for 30 minutes.

Roll out the pastry thinly and use to line 4 lightly buttered individual tartlet tins. Prick all over and bake blind in a preheated oven at 200°C (400°F) mark 6 for 20 minutes until crisp.

Meanwhile prepare the filling. Fillet the trout, removing all the skin and bones, then cut into 5mm (1/4 inch) dice. Place in a bowl, add the remaining ingredients and mix well. Cover and chill until required.

Allow the tartlet cases to cool, then make sure they can easily be removed from the tins but leave in place.

Spoon the trout mixture into the pastry cases and bake at 160°C (325°F) mark 3 for 30-40 minutes until the filling is just set.

LAMB IN A SWEET HERB CRUST

This is by far the best lamb recipe I have ever tried. Although it has a rather fiddly method, it can be prepared in advance and is very easy 'on the night'. Ready-mixed dried Provençal herbs are ideal for the crust, but I have also had good results with fresh herbs — using equal quantities of chopped tarragon and rosemary with a sprinkling of sage. For best results the clarified butter should be just on the point of setting.

2 best ends of lamb or double racks
(16 cutlets in total)
2 carrots, halved
2 onions, halved
125ml (4 fl oz) white wine
4 tomatoes, roughly chopped
bouquet garni (thyme, parsley etc.)
salt and freshly ground pepper
2.25 litres (4 pints) water

Herb Crust:
120ml (8 tbsp) finely crumbled Madeira cake
30ml (2 tbsp) finely chopped parsley
10ml (2 tsp) dried Provençal Herbs
4 cloves garlic, finely chopped
5ml (1 tsp) salt
freshly ground pepper
120ml (8 tbsp) clarified butter

Cut the eye of the meat out of each set of 4 cutlets and reverse. Salvage as much meat as you can from the trimmings, but discard the fat and skin. Separate the cutlet bones and place them in a baking tin with the meat trimmings, carrots and onions. Put into a preheated oven at 230°C

(450ºF) mark 8 for about 20 minutes until browned. Transfer to a stockpot.

Add the wine to the baking tin, stirring up any sediment to deglaze. Add to the stockpot with the tomatoes, bouquet garni, seasoning and water. Bring to a simmer and allow to simmer gently for 2 hours. Strain, then reduce to one third of the original volume or until you have a strong, glossy sauce.

To prepare the crust, mix together the cake crumbs, herbs, garlic and seasoning. Spread the mixture on a large plate or tray. Brush each piece of lamb with the clarified butter and coat evenly with the herb crust. Pat gently to remove any loose crumbs and leave at room temperature for about 20 minutes.

Place the lamb on a rack over a roasting pan and roast in a preheated oven at 200ºC (400ºF) mark 6 for 15 minutes. Remove from the oven and let stand in a warm place for 20 minutes to allow the lamb to develop its "pinkiness". Slice, taking care to disturb the crust as little as possible, and serve with the reduced sauce.

GRATIN DAUPHINOIS

There seem to be as many versions of this classic dish as there are chefs to cook it. When cooked, gratin dauphinois should be creamy with a crusty brown top. If the potatoes are cooked but not browned, finish under a hot grill. Depending on the type of potatoes used, you may find the cooking time is a little longer. King Edwards' seem to give the best results.

450g (1 lb) potatoes
150ml (¹/₄ pint) double cream
150ml (¹/₄ pint) milk
salt and freshly ground pepper
1 clove garlic, crushed
freshly grated nutmeg
40g (1¹/₂ oz) butter

Peel the potatoes and slice them very thinly, using a mandoline if you have one. Plunge the potato slices into a bowl of cold water and leave for a few minutes to remove excess starch. Swirl them around, then drain and dry thoroughly. Heat the cream and milk together until lukewarm.

Layer the potatoes in a buttered gratin dish, sprinkling each layer with seasoning, garlic and a little of the cream/milk mixture. Pour the remaining liquid into the dish. Sprinkle with nutmeg and dot the surface with butter. Bake at the top of a preheated oven at 160ºC (325ºF) mark 3 for about 1¹/₂ hours.

CRUNCHY CARROT PURÉE

This is an informal recipe for my crunchy carrot purée which can be adapted to suit your own taste. You can use a food processor, but unfortunately the texture does not seem to be anything like as good.

450g (1 lb) carrots, roughly chopped
4-5 medium spring onions
25g (1 oz) butter
freshly grated nutmeg
freshly ground pepper

Blanch the carrots in boiling salted water for no longer than 3 minutes; drain thoroughly. Discard most of the green part of the spring onions. Place the spring onions in a blender with the butter, then add the carrots. Season liberally with nutmeg and add pepper to taste.

Blend until all of the chunks of carrot are finely chopped, stirring from time to time. Work until the texture of the purée is to your liking.

PEACHES POACHED WITH LEMON AND BRANDY

This is a deceptively simple dessert which tastes wonderful. I have found that it is sometimes better without all — or even any — of the brandy, so add a little at a time and taste as you go along. You could alternatively substitute an orange liqueur, such as Cointreau or Grand Marnier.

4 large peaches
175g (6 oz) sugar
600ml (1 pint) water
2 large lemons
45ml (3 tbsp) brandy

Immerse the peaches in boiling water for a minute or two to loosen their skins, plunge into cold water, then remove the skins. Halve each peach and remove the stone. Put the sugar and water in a saucepan, dissolve over low heat, then bring to the boil.

Meanwhile trim the ends off the lemons. Slice lemons thinly then add to the syrup. Simmer for 10 minutes, then add the peaches. Simmer until tender; 5-15 minutes depending on ripeness; test with a thin knife and remove each peach when it is ready. When all the peaches have been removed, continue to cook the lemon slices for a further 30 minutes, until transparent. Cool, then stir in the brandy. Pour over the peaches and chill before serving.

REGIONAL HEATS
The South East
Jennifer Twydell • Ashley Davies • Melanie Jappy

Melanie Jappy

While studying the piano and viola at the Royal Scottish Academy of Music and Drama, Melanie's voice was 'discovered' and she worked with George Gordon in Edinburgh and Gita Denies in London with the intention of becoming a professional opera singer. Advised to 'do something else for a few years until your voice matures', Melanie became one of the first women in 130 years to read law at Durham University. She is now continuing her law studies at Guildford. Melanie also skis, rides and plays a mean game of tennis, yet still finds time to involve herself in London's jazz scene.

Melanie Jappy's Menu

Starter
Chicken Livers with Salsa

Main Course
Salmon with Coriander, Plums and Passion Fruit
"Sounds like something Carmen Miranda would order from her hat-maker" Loyd

Dessert
'Floreat Castellum'
(White Chocolate Mousse with Strawberries)

CHICKEN LIVERS WITH SALSA

125g (4 oz) chicken livers
4 shallots
30ml (2 tbsp) olive oil
50g (2 oz) oyster mushrooms

Marinade:
125ml (4 fl oz) sherry
2 cloves garlic, crushed
4 black peppercorns
salt and freshly ground pepper
handful of chopped basil
10 ml (2 tsp) sesame oil

Salsa:
1 red pepper
1/2 green pepper
2 small red chillis (or to taste)
2 shallots
15ml (1 tbsp) capers
15-30ml (1-2 tbsp) olive oil
15ml (1 tbsp) white wine vinegar
juice of 1/2 lime
salt and freshly ground pepper

To Serve:
rocket leaves

Combine all the ingredients for the marinade in a shallow dish. Add the chicken livers and leave to marinate for 3-4 hours or overnight if possible. Drain the livers, then cut into strips.

To make the salsa, remove the core and seeds from the peppers and chillis. Chop the peppers, chilli, shallot and capers very finely. Place in a small bowl. Add the olive oil, vinegar, lime juice and seasoning, mix well and leave to stand.

Cut the shallots into bite-sized pieces. Heat 15ml (1 tbsp) olive oil in a pan and cook the shallots gently for a few minutes. Add the sugar and cook until the shallots are soft and caramelised. Set aside.

Heat the remaining olive oil in the clean pan and sauté the chicken livers for 2-3 minutes. Add the mushrooms and cook for a further 30 seconds. Remove with a slotted spoon and mix with the caramelised shallots. Add the rocket leaves and toss very gently. Serve immediately, with the salsa.

SALMON WITH CORIANDER, PLUMS AND PASSION FRUIT

700g (1¹/₂ lb) salmon fillet, skinned and cut into 4 even-sized portions
50g (2 oz) butter, in pieces
squeeze of lemon juice

Court Bouillon:
1 shallot or ¹/₂ medium onion
2 sticks celery
1 large carrot
300ml (¹/₂ pint) white wine (approximately)
300ml (¹/₂ pint) water (approximately)
10ml (2 tsp) fennel seeds
salt and freshly ground pepper
handful of chopped coriander leaves

Plum and Passion Fruit Sauce:
2-3 passion fruit, halved
4-5 Victoria plums, stoned
10ml (2 tsp) sugar
300ml (¹/₂ pint) water

Garnish:
plum slivers
coriander leaves

For the court bouillon, cut the vegetables into large chunks and place in a pan which will be wide enough to hold the salmon steaks in a single layer. Add the remaining court bouillon ingredients and bring to the boil. Simmer for 20-30 minutes until the stock is a rich yellow colour. Strain off about 90-120ml (6-8 tbsp) and reserve. Add extra wine and water to cover the vegetables if necessary.

Scoop out the seeds and pulp from the passion fruit. Chop the plums and place in a pan with the passion fruit, sugar and water. Cook until soft and jam-like in consistency. Press through a fine nylon sieve to yield a smooth sauce; set aside.

Lay the salmon on the vegetables in the court bouillon pan and allow to half steam/half poach for 4-5 minutes until cooked through, but still springy to touch.

Meanwhile reduce the reserved stock to about half of its original volume, then whisk in the butter, a piece at a time, until you have a smooth yellow sauce. Add lemon juice to taste. Lift a portion of salmon onto the centre of each plate. Spoon the court bouillon sauce on one side of the salmon and the plum and passion fruit sauce on the other side. Decorate the fruit sauce with slivers of plum. Scatter coriander leaves on the yellow sauce. Serve immediately.

'FLOREAT CASTELLUM' (WHITE CHOCOLATE MOUSSE WITH STRAWBERRIES)

I've named this pudding after my college at Durham where I spent three very happy years. The words are from my college song.

100g (3¹/₂ oz) bar white chocolate
40g (1¹/₂ oz) butter
1¹/₂ egg yolks
5 egg whites
30-45ml (2-3 tbsp) whipping cream

Shortbread:
50g (2 oz) butter
25g (1 oz) caster sugar
125g (4 oz) plain flour

To Serve:
125g (4 oz) strawberries
8-10 lychees
75ml (5 tbsp) amaretto liqueur

Melt the chocolate with the butter in a bain-marie (or heatproof bowl over a pan of simmering water). Take off the heat and stir in the egg yolks. Whisk the egg whites until stiff and fold into the chocolate mixture, a spoonful at a time. Whip the cream until soft peaks form, then fold into the mousse. Leave to set.

To make the shortbread, cream the butter and sugar together until light and fluffy. Using your fingers, work in the flour to a soft dough. Be careful not to make it too short or the shortbread will crumble. Lightly roll out to a 5mm (¹/₄ inch) thickness and cut out rounds, or any shape you like. Place on a lightly greased baking sheet and bake in a preheated oven at 180ºC (350ºC) mark 4 for 10-15 minutes until golden. Cool on a wire rack.

Meanwhile, soak the fruit in the liqueur for 20 minutes or longer, depending on how alcoholic you wish it to be! Drain.

Divide the fruit between individual glasses. Top with the chocolate mousse and decorate with the shortbread to serve.

REGIONAL HEATS
THE MIDLANDS
ANGELA JAQUES • GILLIAN STALLARD • JOHNNY WONG

WINNER

ANGELA JAQUES

O riginally from Scotland, Angela has journeyed south to Buckinghamshire and is studying fine art at Amersham College. An intensely practical person, she recently converted a cardboard box of parts into a fully functioning motorbike, and she regularly maintains her middle-aged Saab.

With her husband Peter, Angela organises tastings for the Scottish Malt Whiskey Society which she tutors. But there is some doubt whether the next morning anyone can remember much of what she says!

ANGELA JAQUES' MENU

STARTER
Fish Pleat with Tomato and Herb Sauce

MAIN COURSE
Pigeon Breasts on Perfumed Cabbage
Stoved Potatoes with Thyme

"CABBAGE, JUNIPER AND PIGEON — A MATCH MADE IN HEAVEN" LOYD

"FABULOUS — IT COULD BE IN A 2 OR 3 STAR MICHELIN RESTAURANT, QUITE EASILY" RAYMOND BLANC

DESSERT
Pear Tarts with Fudge Sauce

FISH PLEAT WITH TOMATO AND HERB SAUCE

Honestly, this menu is easy! Just make sure your best friends are the butcher, the greengrocer and the fishmonger. With good suppliers the cooking is the easy part. Get your fishmonger to give you half a tail fillet, 23-30cm (9-12 inches) long, each of salmon, halibut and monkfish. You will be able to cut 4 strips from each — enough for 2 meals for 4 people. Make up the pleats and freeze the ones you don't cook.

Fish Pleats:
2 strips each of halibut, salmon and monkfish, skin removed
30ml (2 tbsp) white wine
1 bay leaf, crushed
1 dill sprig, bruised
pinch of cayenne pepper
freshly ground pepper

Tomato Sauce:
8 very ripe small-medium tomatoes, quartered
2 shallots, finely chopped
1 bay leaf, crushed
1 marjoram, oregano or savory sprig
salt and pepper to taste
45ml (3 tbsp) white wine
grated zest of 1 orange

Herb Sauce:
4 cloves garlic
30ml (2 tbsp) chopped chervil
60ml (4 tbsp) walnut, olive or hazelnut oil

Garnish:
parsley or dill sprigs

Weave the strips of fish into two pleats and place in an ovenproof dish just large enough to hold them in one layer. Add the wine, bay leaf, dill, cayenne and pepper. Cover with foil.

For the tomato sauce, place all the ingredients, except the orange zest, in a small pan and heat until soft and mushy. Press through a sieve, add the orange zest and keep warm.

For the herb sauce, work the garlic, chervil and oil to a thick cream, using a blender, or pestle and mortar.

Cook the fish in a preheated oven at 200°C (400°F) mark 6 for 8-10 minutes; check the monkfish as it takes longest to cook. To assemble, spoon a pool of tomato sauce onto each serving plate. Cut the fish pleats in half and arrange a halved pleat on each plate. Garnish with parsley or dill and serve with a spoonful of herb sauce.

PIGEON BREASTS ON PERFUMED CABBAGE

I like to get ahead of myself on this one and always have stock on hand in the freezer rather than have to boil it up in a hurry, but the instructions for the stock are included below.

4 young pigeons
60ml (4 tbsp) olive, hazelnut or walnut oil
1/2 bottle good red wine
5ml (1 tsp) redcurrant jelly
2 cloves garlic
8-10 juniper berries
pinch of salt
700g (1 1/2 lb) white cabbage, cored and finely shredded
25g (1 oz) chilled butter
30ml (2 tbsp) double cream
30ml (2 tbsp) chopped chervil or flat-leaved parsley

Garnish:
redcurrants or parsley sprigs

Remove the breasts from the pigeons, reserving the carcasses. Marinate in the oil, turning from time to time, for about 2 hours. Chop the pigeon carcasses and brown in a large greased pan. Add water to cover and simmer steadily for 1 1/2 hours. Strain and simmer to reduce to about 300ml (1/2 pint). Add the wine and redcurrant jelly and simmer until reduced to about one third. Set aside.

Pound the garlic and juniper berries with a pinch of salt to a paste, using a pestle and mortar.

Grease a frying pan and sear the pigeon breasts on both sides. Transfer to a greased baking tray and cook in a preheated oven at 230ºC (450ºF) mark 8 for 6 minutes. Cover the cooked pigeon with foil and leave to stand while you cook the cabbage.

Heat a wok or frying pan and melt half of the butter. Add the garlic and juniper paste and stir round to loosen for a few seconds, then increase the heat and add the cabbage. Cook, stirring constantly, until it begins to lose its raw state. Add the cream and lower the heat.

Reheat the red wine sauce and slice the pigeon breasts lengthwise, into thin pink teardrops. Add the chervil or parsley to the cabbage, toss well and place a small mound in the centre of each plate. Arrange the pigeon slices around the castle. Add the remaining butter to the red wine sauce in tiny pieces, shaking the pan as you do so, to thicken the sauce and give it gloss. Trickle the sauce around each castle and decorate with redcurrants or parsley to serve.

STOVED POTATOES WITH THYME

You will need a heavy pan, or cast-iron casserole with a tight-fitting lid for this recipe. The better the fat you use, the better the dish.

1kg (2 lb) egg-sized potatoes, unpeeled
good pinch of sea salt
10ml (2 tsp) chopped thyme
5-10ml (1-2 tsp) goose fat, duck fat or bacon fat

Put all the ingredients into a heavy-based pan, cover tightly and cook over a very low heat, shaking the pan whenever you remember to, for about 1 hour. Try not to peek or you will let out the steam it is cooking in!

PEAR TARTS WITH FUDGE SAUCE

Pastry:
250g (9 oz) plain flour
25g (1 oz) ground almonds
15ml (1 tbsp) icing sugar
150g (5 oz) unsalted butter, diced
pinch of salt
1 egg yolk
15ml (1 tbsp) cold water
15ml (1 tbsp) rum

Confectioner's Custard:
2 egg yolks
30ml (2 tbsp) icing sugar
10ml (2 tsp) plain flour
300ml (1/2 pint) milk
1 vanilla pod

Pear Filling:
4 pears
60ml (4 tbsp) Poire Williem or other fruit
eau-de-vie
60ml (4 tbsp) water
60ml (4 tbsp) sugar

Fudge Sauce:
50g (2 oz) butter
75g (3 oz) Demerara sugar
125ml (4 fl oz) double cream

To make the pastry, put the flour, ground almonds, icing sugar, butter and salt into a blender or food processor and work for 15 seconds until the mixture resembles breadcrumbs. Add the egg yolk, water and rum and whizz for the least amount of time it takes to amalgamate the dough and not a second longer. Turn out and knead briefly and lightly into a sausage shape, 10cm (4 inches) in diameter. Cut in half. Pop one half into a polythene bag and leave to rest in the refrigerator for at least 2 hours. (Freeze the other half for use on another occasion.)

To make the confectioner's custard, in a bowl over a pan of simmering water, whisk the egg yolks and icing sugar until creamy. Remove from the heat and mix in the flour. Heat the milk and vanilla pod until just boiling, then remove the vanilla. Pour a third of the milk onto the egg yolk mixture, stirring until smooth, then add to the remaining milk in the pan. Simmer for 2 minutes, whisking lightly. Remove from the heat and cover the surface of the custard with dampened greaseproof paper to prevent a skin forming.

Peel the pears, halve lengthwise and remove the cores. In a large pan, heat the Poire Williem, water and sugar until dissolved. Add the pears and poach until cooked but still firm. Remove from the syrup and slice crosswise into thin petals. Simmer the syrup until reduced by about half.

Roll out the pastry thinly and use to line 4 individual loose-bottomed flan tins. Prick the bases and bake blind in a preheated oven at 200°C (400°F) mark 6 for 10 minutes.

To make the fudge sauce, put the butter, sugar and cream into a pan. Heat gently until dissolved, then simmer for 4 minutes. Remove from the heat and keep warm.

To assemble, cover the base of each flan case with confectioner's custard and arrange the pear petals in overlapping circles on top. Glaze with the reduced syrup and place the tarts on individual serving plates, with a pool of fudge sauce.

Regional Heats
The Midlands

Angela Jaques • Gillian Stallard • Johnny Wong

Gillian Stallard

Gillian is a physics graduate who has worked in the patent industry for 25 years. For the past 6 years she has been involved with the invention of an intricate digging machine which was recently featured on BBC's Tomorrow's World.

She and her husband live in a romantic water mill in the Oxfordshire countryside. When she is not out walking her dogs beside the canal, Gillian can often be found at her grand piano filling the air with Mozart.

Gillian Stallards' Menu

Starter
Curried Banana Soup

Italian Olive Oil Bread

"If King Kong owned a restaurant this would probably be on the menu" Loyd

Main Course
Pork Fillet with Redcurrant and Port Sauce

Ragoût of Seasonal Vegetables

Dessert
Cardomom Ice Cream with Cinnamon Meringue and Chocolate Sauce

CURRIED BANANA SOUP

15ml (1 tbsp) light olive oil
1 onion, sliced
15ml (1 tbsp) curry powder
scant 25g (1 oz) white rice
1.2 litres (2 pints) chicken stock
2 bananas, roughly chopped
salt and freshly ground pepper
squeeze of lime juice (optional)
chopped coriander leaves to garnish

Heat the olive oil in a pan and cook the onion until softened. Add the curry powder and cook, stirring, for 2 minutes. Stir in the rice, then add the chicken stock. Bring to the boil, cover and simmer gently for 30 minutes. At the end of the cooking time, add the bananas.

Purée the soup in a blender or food processor, then add salt, pepper and lime juice to taste. Garnish with chopped coriander to serve.

ITALIAN OLIVE OIL BREAD

To make sure you have the liquid at the correct temperature, mix two thirds boiling water with one third cold tap water.

450g (1 lb) strong white flour
5ml (l tsp) salt
1 packet easy-mix dried yeast
60ml (4 tbsp) quality olive oil
300ml (¹/₂ pint) water

Sift the flour and salt into a bowl and sprinkle in the dried yeast. Mix 45ml (3 tbsp) olive oil with the water and add to the flour mixture. Mix to a smooth dough and knead for 5 minutes, then leave to rise in a warm place for 1 hour.

Knock back, then flatten and place on an oiled baking sheet. Leave to rise for 15 minutes. Sprinkle the remaining olive oil over the dough and bake in a preheated oven at 200°C (400°F) mark 6 for about 30 minutes. Serve warm.

PORK FILLET WITH REDCURRANT AND PORT SAUCE

2 pork fillets, trimmed
25g (1 oz) butter
2 shallots, finely chopped
15-30ml (1-2 tbsp) finely chopped sage
15 red pepper berries, crushed
pinch of ground mace
salt and freshly ground pepper
12 rashers streaky bacon, rinds removed

Sauce:

1 shallot, finely chopped
15g (¹/₂ oz) butter
125ml (4 fl oz) port
30ml (2 tbsp) redcurrants
15ml (1 tbsp) redcurrant jelly
squeeze of lemon juice (optional)

Cut a slice through each pork fillet, two thirds of the way along the length, so that you have two long pieces and two short pieces. Slit each piece horizontally, but do not cut right through the meat, so that you can open each piece of pork like a book.

Heat the butter in a pan and cook the shallots until softened. Remove from the heat and add the sage, pepper berries, mace and a little salt. Spread half of the mixture on the opened surface of one long piece of pork. Position the two smaller pieces side by side on top. Cover with the rest of the shallot mixture and top with the remaining long piece of pork fillet, so that it looks like a large double-decker sandwich.

Stretch the bacon rashers with the back of a knife and line them up parallel and overlapping one another. Place the pork 'sandwich' on top of the bacon and wrap the bacon tightly round the pork. Place in a baking tin and cook in a preheated oven at 190ºC (375ºF) mark 5 for 1 hour.

For the sauce, cook the shallot in the butter until soft. Add the port and reduce slightly. Add the redcurrants, redcurrant jelly, salt and pepper. Adjust the flavour with lemon juice if required, then sieve.

To serve, cut the pork into slices and serve with the redcurrant and port sauce.

RAGOUT OF SEASONAL VEGETABLES

Tender, young baby vegetables served in a well-flavoured reduced stock. Stir in a spoonful of cream just before serving if you prefer.

12 La Ratte potatoes
125g (4 oz) French beans
125g (4 oz) sugar snap peas
125g (4 oz) baby carrots
125g (4 oz) baby courgettes
125g (4 oz) baby sweetcorn

Vegetable Stock:

1 litre (1³/4 pints) water
1 onion, halved
1 carrot, roughly chopped
1 stick celery
bunch of parsley
1 bay leaf
few peppercorns
salt to taste

First prepare the stock. Place all the ingredients in a large pan and simmer until reduced to about 300ml (¹/2 pint). Strain the stock and return to the pan.

Add the potatoes and cook for 10 minutes, then add all of the remaining vegetables and cook for 4-5 minutes. Serve the vegetables with some of the stock spooned over.

CARDAMOM ICE CREAM WITH CINNAMON MERINGUES AND CHOCOLATE SAUCE

Make sure you use fresh black cardamom seeds. Dried, shrivelled seeds are not suitable.

Ice Cream:
12 cardamom pods
170ml (6 fl oz) milk
3 egg yolks
50g (2 oz) caster sugar
170ml (6 fl oz) double cream

Meringues:
2 egg whites
5ml (1 tsp) ground cinnamon
125g (4 oz) caster sugar

Chocolate Sauce:
50g (2 oz) plain chocolate
30ml (2 tbsp) water

To make the ice cream, extract the seeds from the cardamom pods and grind to a powder. Add the ground cardamom to the milk and heat slowly; do not allow to boil. Beat the egg yolks with the sugar until light. Slowly pour the warm milk on to the egg yolks, beating constantly. Return the mixture to the pan and heat very gently, stirring continuously, until the mixture is thick enough to leave a trail on the back of a wooden spoon. Cool.

Add the cream to the custard. Place in an ice cream machine and churn for about 20 minutes until thick. Alternatively, turn into a freezerproof container and freeze until firm.

To make the cinnamon meringues, whisk the egg whites until soft peaks form. Sift the cinnamon with the sugar, then fold into the egg whites, a little at a time, to yield a smooth glossy meringue. Using a piping bag fitted with a plain nozzle, pipe flat meringues on to a baking sheet lined with non-stick paper. Leave to dry in a very low oven. Cool on a wire rack.

To make the chocolate sauce, melt the chocolate with the water in a double boiler, or heatproof bowl over a pan of simmering water. Stir carefully until smooth.

Serve the ice cream with cinnamon meringues and chocolate sauce.

REGIONAL HEATS
THE MIDLANDS

ANGELA JAQUES • GILLIAN STALLARD • JOHNNY WONG

JOHNNY WONG

Although he lives in Birmingham, at the time the competition was recorded Johnny was studying travel and tourism at Ealing College in London. We're delighted to report that he is now fully qualified and is working as a courier for a Norfolk-based tour company.

When not on the road, Johnny can often be found at his local fencing club elegantly lunging and parrying at his friends with an epée.

JOHNNY WONG'S MENU

STARTER
Broccoli and Almond Mousse with Parma Ham

MAIN COURSE
Supreme of Chicken with Crab and Ginger
Diamond Potatoes
Steamed Mangetout and Baby Corn
"THEY ARE VERY GOOD THESE POTATOES" LOYD

DESSERT
Strawberry Tartlets on a Raspberry Coulis

BROCCOLI AND ALMOND MOUSSE WITH PARMA HAM

350g (12 oz) broccoli, trimmed
3 eggs
150ml (¹/4 pint) double cream
pinch of grated nutmeg
salt and freshly ground pepper
25g (1 oz) flaked almonds, toasted
8 slices Parma ham
salad leaves to serve

Roughly chop the broccoli and steam for 15-20 minutes until tender. Drain and place in a food processor with the eggs. Purée the the mixture until smooth. Stir in the cream and nutmeg and season liberally.

Lightly butter 4 ramekins and sprinkle the almonds on the bases. Carefully fill the ramekins with the broccoli mixture, without disturbing the almonds. Place the ramekins in a roasting tin. Pour enough water into the tin to come one third up the side of the ramekins, as a bain marie. Cover the tin with foil and bake in a preheated oven at 180°C (350°F) mark 4 for 30 minutes.

Turn the mousses out on to individual plates. Arrange 2 slices of Parma ham and a few salad leaves on each plate to serve.

SUPREME OF CHICKEN WITH CRAB AND GINGER

30ml (2 tbsp) olive oil
10ml (2 tsp) grated fresh ginger
175g (6 oz) cooked crabmeat
90ml (6 tbsp) brandy
4 even-sized chicken breasts
125g (4 oz) butter
2 spring onions, shredded
salt and freshly ground pepper
150ml (¹/4 pint) double cream

Heat half the olive oil in a small pan and sweat the ginger for 1 minute, without browning. Add the crabmeat and cook for 2 minutes. Add 30ml (2 tbsp) brandy and cook for 1 minute. Season well and leave to cool.

With a small sharp knife, cut a pocket in each chicken breast. Fill with the crabmeat mixture and secure with cocktail sticks, if necessary to ensure the filling stays in. Heat the remaining oil and half of the butter in a frying pan and sear the chicken breasts on both sides. Transfer each one to a piece of foil, season and top with a piece of spring onion. Wrap the foil around the chicken and seal.

Place the foil parcels in a preheated oven at 200°C (400°F) mark 6 for 15 minutes or until the chicken is tender. Leave in the sealed parcels for 5 minutes.

Meanwhile make the sauce. Heat the remaining brandy in the butter used for searing, then gradually whisk in the cream. Whisk in the remaining butter, a piece at a time, then season.

To serve unwrap the parcels and transfer the chicken breasts to serving plates. Spoon over the sauce and garnish with the remaining shredded spring onion.

DIAMOND POTATOES

A delicious way to roast potatoes. You can enhance the garlic flavour further by adding a sprig or two of herbs to the parcel.

600g (1¹/₄ lb) potatoes
30ml (2 tbsp) olive oil
2 cloves garlic, crushed
salt and freshly ground pepper

Peel the potatoes and cut into 1cm (¹/₂ inch) cubes. Place on a large piece of foil and sprinkle with the olive oil, garlic and seasoning. Fold the foil over the potatoes and secure. Bake in a preheated oven at 190ºC (375ºF) mark 5 for 40 minutes.
Open the foil and bake for a further 30 minutes to brown the potatoes.

STEAMED MANGETOUT AND BABY CORN

If possible, steam the vegetables in separate parchment compartments. It will then be easy to remove each vegetable as it is cooked. The baby corn usually takes a little longer than the mangetout.

225g (8 oz) baby corn cobs
225g (8 oz) mangetout, trimmed
25g (1 oz) butter
5ml (1 tsp) sesame seeds

Halve the baby corn lengthwise. Steam the vegetables for about 5 minutes until tender. Melt the butter and spoon over the vegetables. Sprinkle with sesame seeds to serve.

STRAWBERRY TARTLETS ON A RASPBERRY COULIS

Pastry:
175g (6 oz) plain flour
75g (3 oz) caster sugar
75g (3 oz) butter
1 egg, lightly beaten
a little milk

Crème Pâtissière:
30ml (2 tbsp) flour
50g (2 oz) caster sugar
1 egg yolk
60ml (4 tbsp) milk
60ml (4 tbsp) single cream
5ml (1 tsp) vanilla essence
125g (4 oz) butter

Filling:
350g (12 oz) strawberries, sliced
2.5ml (1/2 tsp) powdered gelatine
100ml (3 fl oz) sweet white wine

Raspberry Coulis:
225g (8 oz) raspberries
75g (3 oz) caster sugar
60ml (4 tbsp) water
a little white wine
60ml (2 fl oz) double cream

To make the pastry, sift the flour and sugar into a bowl and rub in the butter until the mixture resembles fine breadcrumbs. Add the egg and a little milk, mixing to a smooth dough. Knead until smooth, then wrap and chill for 30 minutes.

Roll out the pastry on a lightly floured surface and use to line 4 lightly greased individual flan tins. Bake blind in a preheated oven at 180°C (350°F) mark 4 for 10 minutes. Turn out and leave to cool.

To make the crème pâtissière, mix the flour , sugar and egg yolk together with a little of the milk until smooth.

Put the remaining milk in a pan with the cream and bring to a simmer. Gradually whisk into the flour mixture, return to the pan and cook, whisking until thick and smooth, about 3-4 minutes. Remove from the heat and add the vanilla. Gradually whisk in the butter, a piece at a time, until the crème pâtissière resembles a rich mayonnaise. Leave to cool.

To assemble, spoon some crème pâtissière into each flan case and arrange the strawberries on top. Put the wine in a small basin and sprinkle on the gelatine. Place over a pan of simmering water until dissolved. Leave to cool, then spoon over the fruit. Chill until ready to serve.

To prepare the raspberry coulis, purée the raspberries in a blender or food processor and sieve to remove pips. Heat the sugar and water in a small pan until dissolved, then simmer until reduced to a syrup. Use to sweeten the raspberry purée to taste. If too thick, thin down with a little wine.

To assemble, pour some raspberry coulis on to each plate and tilt the plate to spread it evenly. Lightly whip the cream and use to pipe a decorative border. Place a strawberry tartlet in the centre of each plate.

REGIONAL HEATS

WALES & NORTHERN IRELAND

NICOLE SOCHER • DAPHNE NELSON • TERESA SKIBINSKI

WINNER

NICOLE SOCHER

Nicole, a native of Kentucky, moved to France at the age of six and then to boarding school in England at twelve. After studying politics, philosophy and economics at Oxford, she returned to America, to work on The Washington Post. Now living in Cardiff, Nicole is a features writer with The Western Mail.

Nicole's love of cooking extends to the great outdoors as many a gastronomic dish has come from her trusty Primus during her frequent camping trips in the Welsh mountains.

NICOLE SOCHOR'S MENU

STARTER
Crudités
"VERY ST. TROPEZ" LOYD

MAIN COURSE
Bouillabaisse with Rouille
"OUGHT TO BLOW THE TUSKS OFF AN ELEPHANT" LOYD

DESSERT
Raspberry and Lychee Sorbets with Almond Tuiles
"CREATES AN INCREDIBLY REFRESHING TASTE ON THE PALATE"
PAUL RANKIN

CRUDITÉS

Bouillabaisse is such a rich centrepiece that you don't need an elaborate or sustaining starter. These crudités are simple, light and reminiscent of food served in a French café. For the vinaigrette use 1 part wine vinegar to 4 parts light olive oil and season to taste.

Vegetables:
1/2 medium-sized celeriac
350g (12 oz) fine green beans
1 shallot, finely chopped
3 carrots, grated
1 fennel bulb
2 large or 4 small tomatoes
handful of black olives

Dressing:
about 30ml (2 tbsp) mayonnaise
mustard to taste
15ml (1 tbsp) double cream
about 75ml (5 tbsp) vinaigrette
lemon juice to taste

Garnish:
chopped parsley or chives

Cut the celeriac into julienne strips and blanch in boiling water for a few seconds. Drain, pat dry and toss in a little mayonnaise and mustard. Blanch the green beans in boiling water for 4 minutes; remove while still slightly crisp and refresh in cold water. Drain thoroughly and mix with the shallot, cream and a little vinaigrette.

Toss the carrots in a little vinaigrette, adding a squeeze of lemon juice. Thinly slice the fennel and sprinkle with lemon juice. Slice the tomatoes.

Place a few olives in the centre of each serving plate and arrange the vegetables around them. Spoon a little vinaigrette over the tomatoes and fennel. Sprinkle with chopped herbs to garnish.

BOUILLABAISSE WITH ROUILLE

It is said that it is impossible to make a real bouillabaisse outside the Mediterranean because you can't get the proper fish, but you can achieve a pretty good result. Try to use at least six different varieties and ensure you have a fair amount of authentic fish - such as red or grey mullet, gunard and conger eel. Sea bream, bass, lemon sole, hake and John Dory are all suitable. Include some rascasse if you can get it, plus a good selection of shellfish - crabs, lobster, mussels, etc.

selection of fish and shellfish for
4 generous helpings (see above)

Fish Stock:
125ml (4 fl oz) olive oil
125g (4 oz) onions, chopped
75g (3 oz) leeks, chopped
4 cloves garlic, crushed
230g (8 oz) can chopped tomatoes
1 bottle white wine
1.25 litres (2¹/4 pints) water
2 bay leaves
few parsley sprigs
2.5ml (¹/2 tsp) dried thyme
wedge of fennel bulb
2 large pinches saffron strands,
soaked in water
long strip of pared orange zest
salt and freshly ground pepper
1.5-1.75kg (3¹/2-4 lb) fish bones,
trimmings, shellfish carcasses and cheap
fish

Rouille:
3 fat cloves garlic
¹/2-1 red chilli pepper
¹/2 slices white bread
45ml (3 tbsp) extra virgin olive oil

To Serve:
1 French stick, sliced and toasted
chopped parsley to garnish

First, prepare the fish stock. Heat the olive oil in a large heavy stockpot or flameproof casserole. Add the onions and leeks and cook gently for 5 minutes until softened; do not allow to brown. Add the garlic and tomatoes, increase the heat slightly and cook for 5 minutes. Add the wine, water, herbs, fennel, saffron with liquid, orange zest and seasoning. Bring to the boil, add the fish bones and trimmings, and simmer for 30 minutes. Strain through a sieve, pressing the fish and vegetables to extract as much juice as possible. Reserve this stock.

To prepare the rouille, crush the garlic using a pestle and mortar. Discard the seeds from the chilli, then chop finely. Add to the garlic and pound to a paste. Moisten the bread with a little fish stock, then work into the rouille. Pound in the olive oil, then add enough fish stock to give a smooth, thick paste.

To cook the bouillabisse, bring the fish stock to the boil. Add the fish in order of thickness. Cook, uncovered, transferring the pieces of fish to a serving platter as soon as they are cooked.

Serve the broth in bowls, floating a piece of toasted French bread spread with rouille on top of each one. Sprinkle with chopped parsley and serve with the platter of fish.

RASPBERRY AND LYCHEE SORBETS

Serve the sorbets scooped into individual dishes, with almond tuiles.

Raspberry Sorbet:
450g (1 lb) raspberries
100g (3^1/2 oz) sugar
squeeze of lemon juice
30ml (2 tbsp) double cream

Lychee Sorbet:
425g (15 oz) can lychees in syrup
squeeze of lime juice

To make the raspberry sorbet, sprinkle the raspberries with the sugar and leave to macerate for 2 hours. Purée in a blender or food processor, then press through a stainless steel sieve. Add lemon juice to taste and the cream. Freeze in a sorbetière.

To make the lychee sorbet, purée the lychees with their syrup in a blender or food processor, then add lime juice to taste and freeze in a sorbetière.

Note: If you do not have a sorbetière, turn each mixture into a freezerproof container and freeze until almost firm. Remove and whisk thoroughly. Return to the container and freeze until firm.

ALMOND TUILES

The secret of these delicate tuiles is to make thin perfect circles of batter on the baking sheets otherwise they spread into odd shapes during baking.

25g (1 oz) butter, melted
50g (2 oz) icing sugar
25g (1 oz) plain flour
15ml (1 tbsp) grated lemon rind
1 egg white
25g (1 oz) flaked almonds
Icing sugar for dusting

Whisk together the melted butter, icing sugar, flour, lemon rind and egg white to a smooth batter. Drop teaspoonfuls of batter on to greased baking sheets, spacing well apart; allow four to each baking sheet. Carefully spread into perfect thin circles and sprinkle with almonds.

Bake, one sheet at a time, in a preheated oven at 200°C (400°F) mark 6 for about 5 minutes until lightly browned. Quickly remove from the baking sheet, using a palette knife, and drape over the curve of a rolling pin. Allow to cool, before removing. Sprinkle with icing sugar to serve.

REGIONAL HEATS

WALES & NORTHERN IRELAND

NICOLE SOCHER • DAPHNE NELSON • TERESA SKIBINSKI

DAPHNE NELSON

Daphne Nelson is *MasterChef's* first contestant from Northern Ireland. She lives in Belfast with her husband Ken, a consultant at Ulster Hospital, and her two daughters — both vegetarians. Daphne, too, works part-time in the hospital looking after the mobile shop and library.

A keen linguist, Daphne attends regular French discussion groups and dashes off to Europe as often as possible, particularly for the golf. When at home, she enjoys the challenge of the Royal Belfast golf course.

DAPHNE NELSON'S MENU

STARTER
Avocado and Roquefort Puffs with Gooseberry Sauce

MAIN COURSE
Sole Fillets Stuffed with Smoked Salmon Mousse
Lemon Rice Timbales
Bâtons of Courgette and Carrot

DESSERT
Raspberry and Cinnamon Torte with Raspberry Sauce
"VERY, VERY, VERY, VERY, VERY GOOD" LOYD
"A STUNNER" PAUL RANKIN

AVOCADO AND ROQUEFORT PUFFS WITH GOOSEBERRY SAUCE

These delicious puffs work equally well with filo or puff pastry.

2 sheets filo pastry or 200g (7 oz) packet puff pastry
melted butter for brushing (optional)

Filling:
1 large ripe avocado
125g (4 oz) Roquefort cheese

Gooseberry Sauce:
450g (1 lb) gooseberries
a few elderflowers (if available)
15ml (1 tbsp) honey
squeeze of lemon juice

To Garnish:
salad leaves tossed in a walnut oil vinaigrette

For the filling, peel, halve and stone the avocado, then mash the flesh with the Roquefort.

If using filo pastry, cut out eight 10cm (4 inch) squares. Brush with melted butter and place pairs of squares on top of one another. Place a spoonful of filling in the centre and fold into small parcels.

If using puff pastry, roll out and cut four 10cm (4 inch) squares. Divide the filling between them and fold into triangles, sealing the edges well.

Place on a greased baking sheet and bake in a preheated oven at 200°C (400°F) mark 6 until golden brown; allow 5-10 minutes for filo puffs; 10-15 minutes for puff pastry ones.

Meanwhile make the gooseberry sauce. Place the gooseberries, elderflowers and honey in a pan and cook for about 10 minutes until pulpy. Discard the elderflowers, cool slightly, then place in a blender or food processor and work until smooth. Press through a sieve then taste and add some lemon juice if the sauce needs to be sharper.

Serve the puffs garnished with salad leaves tossed in a walnut oil vinaigrette, and accompanied by the gooseberry sauce.

Sole Fillets Stuffed with Smoked Salmon Mousse

125g (4 oz) smoked salmon
125g (4 oz) salmon fillet
1 egg white
200ml (8 fl oz) single cream
salt and freshly ground pepper
5ml (1 tsp) chopped dill
8 sole fillets
45ml (3 tsp) dry white wine
few dill sprigs
5ml (1 tsp) tomato purée
lemon juice to taste
dill sprigs to garnish

Cut half of the smoked salmon into fine strips and reserve for garnish. Chop the remaining smoked salmon and the fresh salmon, then place in a blender or food processor with the egg white, 30ml (2 tbsp) cream and a pinch of salt. Stir in the chopped dill. Lay the sole fillets on a board, sprinkle with salt and pepper, then divide the salmon mixture between them. Roll up the fillets and place in a buttered shallow ovenproof dish. Pour over the wine and add the dill sprigs. Cover with foil and cook in a preheated oven at 180°C (350°F) mark 4 for about 20 minutes.

Carefully lift out the fish rolls and keep warm. Pour the cooking juices into a saucepan and boil rapidly until reduced by about half. Add the remaining cream and the tomato purée, stir well and boil for a few minutes. Season carefully, possibly adding a little lemon juice.

To serve, cut each rolled fillet in half and arrange 4 halves on each plate, cut side up. Pour over the sauce, then garnish with the reserved smoked salmon strips and dill sprigs.

Lemon Rice Timbales

225g (8 oz) Basmatic rice
1 bay leaf
2.5ml ($^1/_2$ tsp) turmeric
2.5cm (1 inch) piece fresh root ginger, grated
juice of $^1/_2$ lemon
50g (2 oz) pistachio nuts, chopped

Wash the rice thoroughly and put into a saucepan. Add twice the volume of water, the bay leaf, turmeric and ginger. Bring to the boil, cover and simmer for 8-10 minutes until cooked. Add the lemon juice and chopped nuts. Discard the bay leaf.

Gently press the rice into 4 oiled ramekins, then carefully turn out on to warmed plates and serve.

RASPBERRY AND CINNAMON TORTE
WITH RASPBERRY SAUCE

This cinnamon scented torte is particularly good served warm, with a mixture of lightly whipped and thick creamy Greek yogurt.

150g (5 oz) soft margarine
150g (5 oz) caster sugar
150g (5 oz) ground almonds
150g (5 oz) self-raising flour
5ml (1 tsp) ground cinnamon
1 egg
225g (8 oz) raspberries

Raspberry Sauce:
225g (8 oz) raspberries
15ml (1 tbsp) icing sugar
5ml (1 tsp) lemon juice

To Serve:
icing sugar and ground cinnamon for dusting
whipped cream and Greek yogurt

Place the margarine, caster sugar, ground almonds, flour, cinnamon and egg in a bowl. Beat thoroughly to mix. Spread half of the mixture in a greased and base-lined 22cm (8^1/2 inch) spring-release cake tin and flatten slightly, using a fork. Sprinkle the raspberries over the mixture and dot the remaining torte mixture on top so that it almost covers the fruit.

Stand the tin on a baking sheet and bake in a preheated oven at 180°C (350°F) mark 4 for about 45 minutes, covering lightly with foil if the top is becoming too brown. When cooked, the torte will feel just firm and slightly springy. Leave in the tin to cool for about 1 hour.

Meanwhile prepare the raspberry sauce. Purée the raspberries in a food processor or blender with the icing sugar and lemon juice, then seive to remove the pips.

Turn out the cooled torte and dust with icing sugar sifted with cinnamon. Serve warm, accompanied by the raspberry sauce and cream mixed with yogurt.

REGIONAL HEATS

WALES & NORTHERN IRELAND

NICOLE SOCHER • DAPHNE NELSON • TERESA SKIBINSKI

TERESA SKIBINSKI

Originally from Modena in Italy, Teresa has lived in Swansea with her husband, David, who is a genetic scientist at the university, for 17 years. They have two chidren, and the family love the wonderful countryside of the Gower Peninsular.

Teresa teaches Italian at the local secondary school, and in the village hall on Sunday mornings. She is an enthusiastic art collector with works by John Piper and Kerry Richards as well as the best local artists, and she channels her own creativity into tapestry and her splendid garden.

TERESA SKIBINSKI'S MENU

STARTER
Garganelli with Mushroom Sauce
"VERY NICE — VERY EARTHY" JEAN SHRIMPTON

MAIN COURSE
Guinea Fowl Breasts with Madeira Sauce
Glazed Carrots
Sautéed Leeks
"GUINEA FOWL...CHICKEN WITH A UNIVERSITY EDUCATION" LOYD

DESSERT
Strawberry Mousse with Strawberry Sauce

GARGANELLI WITH MUSHROOM SAUCE

This is a very old fashioned pasta dish, featuring garganelli - handmade macaroni. To prepare it you need a wooden tool called a *pettine* or comb. At home in Italy we use an old loom reed. You lay a pasta square on the comb and roll a dowel over it. Around the dowel you will have a single pasta tube with a ridged surface. This process seems time consuming, but the texture of the pasta justifies the effort.

Pasta Dough:
200g (7 oz) white flour (soft wheat flour - type oo)
2-3 eggs

Mushroom Sauce:
50g (2 oz) dried porcini (ceps)
15ml (1 tbsp) olive oil
1 clove garlic, crushed
125g (4 oz) oyster mushrooms
salt and freshly ground pepper
125ml (4 fl oz) double cream
100g (3¹/₂ oz) freshly grated Parmesan cheese

To prepare the pasta dough, put the flour and eggs into a food processor and work until smooth. Put the dough in a polythene bag and leave to rest for about 30 minutes. Roll out the dough as thinly as possible and cut out 2.5cm (1 inch) squares. Roll each pasta square diagonally around a thin wooden dowel over the wooden comb to create a ridged pattern. Slide each pasta tube off the dowel and leave to dry.

For the mushroom sauce, soak the porcini in warm water to cover for 2 hours. Drain, reserving the liquid. Chop the porcini. Heat the olive oil in a frying pan and add the garlic, porcini and oyster mushrooms. Heat gently, adding the reserved soaking liquid. Season with salt and simmer until the liquid has evaporated.

Cook the pasta in boiling salted water until *al dente*; this will take only 20 seconds - 1 minute. Drain and add to the mushrooms, with the cream, Parmesan and pepper. Toss over high heat, then serve immediately.

GUINEA FOWL BREASTS WITH MADEIRA SAUCE

4 guinea fowl breasts
300ml ($^1/_2$ pint) homemade chicken stock
100g (3$^1/_2$ oz) butter
15ml (1 tbsp) double cream
salt and freshly ground pepper
few drops of lemon juice (optional)

Marinade:
1 glass Madeira wine
30ml (2 tbsp) olive oil
few black peppercorns, crushed
sea salt
1 clove garlic, crushed
1 onion, sliced
1 stick celery, chopped
few juniper berries
few thyme sprigs
1-2 bay leaves

Trim the guinea fowl, removing the skin. Combine the ingredients for the marinade in a shallow dish. Add the guinea fowl breasts, turn to coat and leave to marinate for 2-3 hours, turning occasionally. Remove the guinea fowl, strain the marinade and reserve.

Bring the stock to the boil in a pan and simmer until reduced by half.

Heat the butter in a large shallow pan, add the guinea fowl breasts and cook for 3-4 minutes on each side. Remove with a slotted spoon and keep warm.

Pour out the butter into a bowl, then add the reserved marinade to the pan. Simmer to reduce, then add the reduced stock and whisk in the cream. Reduce until syrupy, adding more butter if necessary to give a shiny sauce. Season to taste and add lemon juice if desired.

Serve the guinea fowl breasts with the Madeira sauce.

GLAZED CARROTS

450g (1 lb) baby carrots
40g (1$^1/_2$ oz) unsalted butter
pinch of caster sugar
salt and freshly ground pepper

Trim and clean the carrots. Melt the butter in a large pan, add the carrots in a single layer, with the sugar and salt. Add just enough cold water to cover and bring to the boil. Simmer for about 10 minutes. Taste and, if the carrots are almost cooked, reduce the liquid until the carrots are glazed.

Season the carrots with pepper to taste and serve.

SAUTÉED LEEKS

450g (1 lb) leeks
15ml (1 tbsp) olive oil
25g (1 oz) unsalted butter
salt and freshly ground pepper

Trim and clean the leeks, removing most of the green part of the leaves (use these for stock). Cut into rounds.

Heat the olive oil and butter in a pan, add the leeks and cook until softened. Season to taste and serve.

STRAWBERRY MOUSSE WITH STRAWBERRY SAUCE

I first made this dessert for my husband 17 years ago and it has been his favourite ever since!

450g (1 lb) strawberries
260g (9¹/2 oz) caster sugar
100ml (3¹/2 fl oz) crème de framboise liqueur
1 packet powdered gelatine
45ml (3 tbsp) orange juice, warmed
2 egg whites
5ml (1 tsp) lemon juice
200ml (7 fl oz) whipping cream

Strawberry Sauce:
225g (8 oz) strawberries
100g (3¹/2 oz) caster sugar
juice of ¹/2 lemon
crème de framboise liqueur to taste

To prepare the mousse, put the strawberries in a dish. Sprinkle with 200g (7 oz) sugar and the framboise liqueur. Leave to macerate for at least 30 minutes. Purée the mixture in a blender or food processor, then pass through a nylon sieve. Sprinkle the gelatine on to the warm orange juice to dissolve, then add to the strawberry purée.

Whisk the egg whites until soft peaks form, then whisk in the remaining 60g (2¹/2 oz) sugar, to give a firm meringue. Add the lemon juice.

In a separate cold bowl, whip the cream until it begins to thicken and the whisk leaves a trail. Carefully fold in the cold strawberry mixture, then fold in the meringue. Spoon into 4 ramekins and level the surfaces. Place in the coldest part of the refrigerator to set.

To make the strawberry sauce, purée the fruit and sugar together in a blender or food processor, then press through a fine sieve. Add the lemon juice and framboise liqueur to taste.

To serve, carefully unmold each mousse on to a chilled dessert plate. Pour the strawberry sauce around each mousse and serve.

REGIONAL HEATS
LONDON
JO EITEL • BRUCE HYMAN • KATE WHITEMAN

WINNER

JO EITEL

Jo was particularly pleased to succeed in *MasterChef 1991* as she hopes soon to move to France with her fiancé, Stuart, and open a small restaurant. At the moment she lives in London's fashionable docklands and is a top salesperson with an office systems company.

A daily dose of aerobics keeps Jo fit. She also has a fine collection of trophies for clay pigeon shooting, a sport she took up less than two years ago.

JO EITEL'S MENU

STARTER
Nuggets of Langoustine in Basil Parcels
"OH GOSH, THAT'S REALLY DELICIOUS"   LOYD
"YOU CAN HAVE ME AT YOUR HOUSE ANYTIME"   LYNDA BELLINGHAM

MAIN COURSE
Rack of Lamb in a Provençal Herb Crust with
Wild Mushroom Sauce
Papillote of Roast Vegetables
"VERY GOOD IDEA"   ANTONIO CARLUCCIO

DESSERT
Apple and Puff Pastry Love Hearts
"I COULD BECOME A PUDDING PERSON"   LYNDA BELLINGHAM

NUGGETS OF LANGOUSTINE IN BASIL PARCELS

24 fresh langoustines
20 large basil leaves, with stems
30ml (2 tbsp) chopped chervil leaves
600ml (1 pint) vegetable stock

Ginger Sauce:
2 shallots, finely chopped
30ml (2 tbsp) white wine
45ml (3 tbsp) white wine vinegar
5ml (1 tsp) coarsely ground black pepper
40ml (scant 3 tbsp) double cream
250g (9 oz) butter (preferably Jersey
butter for its rich colour), in pieces
15-30ml (1-2 tbsp) chopped fresh
root ginger
salt

Salad:
4 small bunches of lamb's lettuce (corn
salad)
handful of rocket leaves
handful of radicchio leaves
30ml (2 tbsp) olive oil
1.25ml (1/4 tsp) Dijon mustard
10ml (2 tsp) white wine vinegar
salt and freshly ground pepper

First make the ginger sauce. Place the shallots, wine, vinegar and pepper in a saucepan. Bring to the boil and simmer until the liquid has reduced by two thirds. Gradually whisk in the cream, butter and ginger and allow to simmer very gently for 5-10 minutes. Pass the sauce through a sieve into a basin. Check seasoning and stand over a pan of simmering water until ready to use.

Steam 4 whole langoustines for approximately 4 minutes, until cooked. Meanwhile peel the remaining langoustines, leaving 1cm (1/2 inch) shell on the tail ends. Wash the peeled langoustines, then pat dry. Sprinkle with salt, pepper and chervil.

To prepare each nugget, lay a peeled langoustine across the width of each basil leaf. Pierce a tiny hole about 1cm (1/2 inch) from the tip of the leaf, wrap the leaf around the langoustine and tuck the stem end through the hole. Repeat to make 20 nuggets in total. Place the nuggets in the top of a steamer. Bring the vegetable stock to the boil in the bottom of the steamer and steam the nuggets for 3-4 minutes until the langoustines are cooked, adding the whole langoustines for the final 2 minutes to heat through.

Meanwhile prepare the salad. Combine the salad leaves. To make the dressing, place the olive oil, mustard, wine vinegar and seasoning in a screw-topped jar and shake thoroughly to combine. Toss the salad leaves in the dressing.

To serve, arrange the salad leaves on individual plates. Position the langoustine nuggets in a circle on each plate and spoon over some of the ginger sauce. Place a whole langoustine in the centre of each circle. Serve immediately, with the remaining sauce.

RACK OF LAMB IN A PROVENÇAL HERB CRUST WITH WILD MUSHROOM SAUCE

3 best ends of lamb, each with 8 cutlets
120ml (8 tbsp) brioche crumbs
10ml (2 tsp) dried Provençal herbs
30ml (2 tbsp) finely chopped parsley
4 garlic cloves, finely chopped
salt and freshly ground pepper
60ml (4 tbsp) clarified butter or olive oil

Sauce:
450ml (³/₄ pint) demi-glace (see page 49)
22ml (1¹/₂ tbsp) dried ceps
15ml (1 tbsp) Madeira
125g (4 oz) small pied de mouton mushrooms

Keeping the fillet attached to the bone, trim as much of the fat from the lamb as possible. Scrape the bones to remove all the fat and sinew.

Mix together the brioche crumbs, herbs, garlic, salt and pepper. Brush the lamb with the clarified butter or olive oil. Sprinkle the mixture over the lamb and gently pat on to the meat, covering all of the flesh.

Place the lamb on the rack over a roasting tin and roast in a preheated oven at 200°C (400°F) mark 6 for 20-25 minutes.

Meanwhile make the sauce. Bring the demi-glace to the boil, add the ceps and simmer until the liquid has reduced by about half. Add the Madeira and reduce until it coats the back of a spoon. Place the sauce in a bain marie or a heatproof bowl over a pan of boiling water. Stir in the pied de mouton and leave to cook gently for 10 minutes.

To serve, spoon the pied de mouton into the centre of 4 warmed plates. Slice the lamb between each bone and arrange the cutlets in a circle around the mushrooms,with the ribs crossing over them. Spoon a little of the sauce over the mushrooms and serve.

DAPHNE NELSON'S DESSERT

Raspberry and Cinnamon Torte with Raspberry Sauce

KATE WHITEMAN'S MAIN COURSE

Prince of Wales Salmon
Green Lentils with Mild Mustard Sauce
Minted Sugar Snap Peas
Steamed Broccoli

DEMI GLACE

I have given a separate recipe for this, as it is also used in my semi-final and final main courses (pages 151 and 172).
Marrow bones and knuckles are ideal for the stock.

Veal Stock:
1kg (2 lb) fresh veal bones, finely chopped
75g (3 oz) clarified butter
30ml (2 tbsp) clear honey
30ml (2 tbsp) groundnut oil
4 carrots, coarsely chopped
1 onion, coarsely chopped
1 small leek, white part only, halved
1 stick celery
2 shallots, finely chopped
2 cloves garlic, finely sliced
230g (8 oz) can peeled plum tomatoes
50g (2 oz) large mushrooms, finely chopped
1 thyme sprig
1 parsley sprig
1 bay leaf

To Finish:
3 egg whites
15ml (1 tbsp) dried Provençal herbs

Brush the veal bones with the clarified butter and honey and place in a roasting tin. Roast in a preheated oven at 220°C (425°F) mark 7 for about 45 minutes until nicely browned.

Heat the oil in a large heavy-based stainless steel pan, add the vegetables and cook gently until softened.

Add the bones to the vegetables. Add a little water to the roasting tin, stirring to deglaze, then add to the vegetables. Pour in about 3 litres (5 pints) water, bring to the boil and skim. Add the thyme, parsley and bay leaf, then simmer for 4-5 hours. Remove the bones and strain the stock.

To make the demi glace, measure 1 litre ($1^3/4$ pints) veal stock into a clean pan. Whisk in the egg whites and simmer for 10 minutes, then strain through a muslin-lined stainless steel sieve into another pan. Tie the herbs in a muslin bouquet, add to the beautifully clear stock and simmer until reduced to 450ml ($^3/4$ pint). Now you have the demi glace.

Papillote of Roast Vegetables

Leave the papillotes for your guests to open so that they can enjoy the full aroma.

1 medium fennel bulb
1 stick celery
1 courgette
4 thick asparagus spears
4 baby carrots, with leaves
4 baby waxy potatoes (preferably pink fir apple variety)
4 button onions
4 large dried morels, pre-soaked and drained
60ml (4 tbsp) clarified butter
15ml (1 tbsp) sugar
15ml (1 tbsp) salt
4 tarragon sprigs
4 thyme sprigs
4 cloves garlic
20 black peppercorns

Cut the fennel bulb into quarters. Cut the celery into four 7.5cm (3 inch) strips. Cut the courgette into four 7.5cm (3 inch) lengths. Trim the asparagus spears to 7.5cm (3 inch) lengths. Place all the vegetables in a bowl. Melt the clarified butter and stir in the sugar and salt. Pour over the vegetables and turn to coat them evenly.

Take four A4 sheets of greaseproof paper, fold each one in half, then open again. Place each portion of vegetables at one side of the fold. Add the herbs, garlic and 5 peppercorns per parcel. Fold the greaseproof paper over the vegetables. To make the papillotes, refer to the diagram on page 171. Place on a baking sheet and cook in a preheated oven at 200°C (400°F) mark 6 for 20 minutes. Serve on warmed side plates.

APPLE AND PUFF PASTRY LOVE HEARTS

For these I use Cox's Orange Pippins and thick Tasmanian honey which has a delightful bouquet. I cut out the pastry shapes with a knife, but you can purchase heart-shaped cutters from good kitchenware shops.

225g (8 oz) packet puff pastry (chilled)
1¹/₂ dessert apples
squeeze of lemon juice
beaten egg to glaze
melted honey to glaze

Sauce:
30ml (2 tbsp) honey
150ml (¹/₄ pint) double cream
45-60ml (3-4 tbsp) Calvados

Lightly roll out the pastry to a 5mm (¹/₄ inch) thickness and cut 4 heart shapes, each about 7.5 x 7.5cm (3 x 3 inches). Leave to rest for 10 minutes. Place on a baking sheet.

Meanwhile, peel, core and thinly slice the apples to approximately 2mm (¹/₈ inch) thickness. Sprinkle with lemon juice to prevent browning. Carefully layer the apple slices on the pastry hearts, working from the sides towards the centre and overlapping each slice by two thirds.

Brush the exposed pastry edges with egg. Brush the apples (gently so as not to dislodge your wonderful workmanship) with a little melted honey. Bake in a preheated oven at 220ºC (425ºF) mark 7 for 20-30 minutes until the pastry has risen and the apple topping golden brown.

Meanwhile make the sauce. Melt the honey in a saucepan and heat until bubbling. Allow to boil for 1 minute. Remove from the heat and stir in the cream; it may splutter a little. Return to the heat and cook until the sauce turns a caramel colour. Add the Calvados, a little at a time, tasting as you go. Neither the honey nor the Calvados should steal the show, but they should be a delicious double act.

To serve, place each apple love heart in the centre of a large plate and pour a circle of sauce around. Serve, eat and enjoy!

REGIONAL HEATS

LONDON

JO EITEL • BRUCE HYMAN • KATE WHITEMAN

BRUCE HYMAN

Bruce is a theatre producer with a long string of hits behind him, and productions of Don Giovanni and The Marriage of Figaro in rehearsal. He is also an avid and talented skier, and a member of the 1992 Olympic Committee.

Friday nights find Bruce eyes down in his Hampstead home, playing serious poker; other nights it is the piano; or maybe a pen and ink drawing of his girlfriend *sa copine* who lends her title to his crab-filled ravioli.

BRUCE HYMAN'S MENU

STARTER
Crab and Ginger Ravioli with Sauce de ma Copine

MAIN COURSE
Lamb Cassis
Creamed Parsley
Confit of Baby Onions
Sautéed Chicory

DESSERT
Tarte Tatin
Crème Fraîche Vanilla Ice Cream

CRAB AND GINGER RAVIOLI WITH SAUCE DE MA COPINE

Use the thinnest sheets of fresh pasta you can find for these delicate ravioli. Your local Italian delicatessen is probably the best place to buy them.

225g (8 oz) very thin sheet fresh plain pasta
225g (8 oz) very thin sheet fresh green pasta

Filling:
100g (3¹/2 oz) freshly cooked crabmeat
100g (3¹/2 oz) sole fillets, skinned
15ml (1 tbsp) tomato concassé (see note)
15ml (1 tbsp) mascarpone or double cream
handful of coriander leaves, shredded
10ml (2 tsp) shredded fresh root ginger
1 egg, beaten
salt and freshly ground pepper
10-15ml (2-3 tsp) grapefruit juice (to taste)

Sauce de ma Copine:
75ml (3 fl oz) ginger wine
150ml (¹/4 pint) white wine
75ml (3 fl oz) white wine vinegar
2 shallots, chopped
2 bay leaves
10 black peppercorns
handful of fresh root ginger peelings
150g (5 oz) unsalted butter
10-15ml (2-3 tsp) grapefruit juice (to taste)

To Serve:
1 small leek
a little olive oil
10ml (2 tsp) tomato concassé (see note)

First prepare the sauce. Place all of the ingredients, except the butter and grapefruit juice, in a saucepan. Bring to the boil and boil vigorously until reduced to about one sixth of the original volume. Strain through a fine-meshed conical sieve into a heatproof bowl and whisk in the butter, a little at a time. Add grapefruit juice to taste and keep warm over a pan of simmering water.

Lay the pasta on a work surface and cut out large circles, using a 7.5cm (3 inch) pastry cutter. Dampen the pasta circles.

For the filling, place all of the ingredients in a food processor or blender and work until the mixture is evenly blended and of a dropping consistency. Check the seasoning.

Place a heaped teaspoonful of filling on one half of each circle. Fold the other half over and press the edges together to seal, using your fingers or the blunt edge of a slightly smaller pastry cutter (than the one used for cutting out circles). Cook the ravioli in a large pan of boiling salted water until *al dente*, about 4 minutes.

Meanwhile cut the leek into fine julienne strips and sauté in a little olive oil until crispy. Season with salt to taste.

To serve, drain the ravioli. Pour the sauce de ma copine on to individual serving plates. Add the ravioli and garnish with tiny spoonfuls of tomato concassé and leek julienne. Serve immediately.

Note: For the tomato concassé; simply peel a few ripe tomatoes, by plunging into a bowl of boiling water for about 30 seconds, then removing the skins. Quarter the tomatoes, discard the seeds, then finely chop the flesh and use as concassé.

LAMB CASSIS

For this exquisite dish, ask your butcher to cut out the eye of the meat, or noisette, from each set of cutlets, in one piece. The bones are ideal for making the stock.

2 best end of lamb fillets, trimmed (see above)
1 clove garlic, cut into slivers
1 rosemary branch
coarse sea salt
pinch of flour
5ml (1 tsp) Dijon mustard
45ml (3 tbsp) olive oil
4 shallots, peeled
75ml (3 fl oz) crème de cassis

Lamb Stock:
1kg (2 lb) lamb bones, roasted
2 onions, quartered
1 bay leaf
salt and freshly ground pepper
1/2 bottle Madeira
1/2 bottle red wine
1/4 bottle crème de cassis

Cassis Juice:
450g (1 lb) blackcurrants
60ml (4 tbsp) icing sugar
75ml (3 fl oz) crème de cassis
60ml (4 tbsp) blackcurrant jam
240ml (7 1/2 fl oz) blackcurrant vinegar

First prepare the stock. Place all of the ingredients in a large saucepan and add sufficient water to cover. Bring to the boil, then simmer until reduced to a quarter of the original volume. Strain and reserve.

For the cassis juice, heat the blackcurrants and icing sugar together in a pan, stirring, until the mixture is bubbling. Strain through a fine-meshed conical sieve, return to the pan and add the cassis. Heat the blackcurrant jam in another pan until bubbling, then add the vinegar, stirring to deglaze. Reduce to a thick syrup, then stir into the cassis mixture.

For the sauce, measure the cassis juice and add 3 parts lamb stock to 1 part cassis juice.

To prepare the lamb, spike each fillet in 4 places and insert a tiny sliver of garlic in each hole. Make another 4 incisions and insert tiny rosemary sprigs. Sprinkle liberally with crunchy salt. Dust very lightly with the flour. Blend the mustard with 15ml (1 tbsp) olive oil and spread along the top of each fillet and liberally over the ends.

Place the meat in a roasting tin and add the shallots. Sprinkle the shallots with the remaining olive oil, a little salt and a few rosemary sprigs. Roast in a preheated oven at 190°C (375°F) mark 5 for 9 minutes. Wrap the lamb in foil and let stand for 12-13 minutes. Meanwhile deglaze the pan juices with the cassis, stirring to scrape up the sediment. Strain and mix with the sauce; reheat.

To serve, cut the lamb into 5mm (1/4 inch) slices, discarding the end pieces. Arrange in an overlapping circle, with the creamed parsley in the centre. Spoon over a little of the sauce; serve the remainder separately.

CREAMED PARSLEY

50g (2 oz) parsley sprigs
60ml (4 tbsp) double cream
freshly grated nutmeg
salt and freshly ground pepper

Remove the stalks from the parsley and blanch the leaves in boiling salted water for 1 minute. Drain thoroughly and chop very finely in a food processor or blender. Add 45ml (3 tbsp) cream with grated nutmeg, salt and pepper to taste.

Whizz for 2-3 seconds (no longer or you will whip the cream), then return to the pan and heat through. Add a little more cream if it looks too stodgy. Serve hot, with the lamb.

CONFIT OF BABY ONIONS

20 baby onions (unpeeled)
coarse sea salt
pinch of caster sugar
2 pinches of mixed dried herbs

Put the unpeeled baby onions on a large sheet of foil and sprinkle with the salt, sugar and dried herbs. Fold the foil over the onions to enclose and seal the parcel by folding in the ends and pinching the edges together. Cook in a preheated oven at 190°C (375°F) mark 5 for 35 minutes. To serve, unwrap and snip off the rounder ends of the onions to make them easier to peel.

SAUTÉED CHICORY

4 heads chicory
30-45ml (2-3 tbsp) extra virgin olive oil
pinch of caster sugar
coarse sea salt
4 rosemary sprigs

Split each head of chicory lengthwise. Heat the olive oil in a frying pan, add the chicory, sugar, salt to taste, and rosemary. Cook, turning constantly, until the chicory is slightly softened and tinged brown at the edges. Serve immediately.

TARTE TATIN

For this French apple tart, you will need an 18cm (7 inch) tatin pan or flan tin, which is about 4cm (1½ inches) deep. The pastry quantity is sufficient to make 4 tarts; freeze the other portions for use on other occasions.

Pastry:
200g (7 oz) plain flour
5ml (1 tsp) ground almonds
100g (3½ oz) butter
50g (2 oz) sugar
1 egg, lightly beaten
5ml (1 tsp) double cream

Filling:
3 dessert apples
25g (1 oz) butter
75g (3 oz) caster sugar
30ml (2 tbsp) Calvados

To make the pastry, put the flour and ground almonds in a food processor and mix for a few seconds. Add the butter, in pieces, and process briefly until the mixture resembles fine breadcrumbs. Turn into a bowl. If you do not have a food processor, mix together the flour and ground almonds and rub in the butter using your fingertips.

Stir in the sugar, then add the egg and cream and mix together, using your fingers, until the dough binds together; avoid over-kneading. Divide into 4 equal portions, wrap in cling film and leave to rest in the refrigerator for about 30 minutes.

Meanwhile prepare the filling. Peel, quarter and core the apples. Cut the butter into tiny pieces and dot over the base of a lightly buttered 18cm (7 inch) tatin pan. Sprinkle the sugar evenly over the top and place over a low heat until the mixture starts to caramelize, stirring very gently if necessary; avoid stirring too much otherwise lumps of caramel will form. When the mixture is light brown in colour, with a treacle-like consistency, remove from the heat and immediately arrange the apple quarters in a circle on top, placing 2 quarters in the centre. Set aside to cool.

Take a portion of pastry and roll out on a lightly floured surface to a circle large enough to cover the tatin pan. Sprinkle the Calvados evenly over the apples and position the pastry on top. Fold back any excess pastry, rather than trim, so that it fits neatly. Make 4 equal slits in the pastry around the edge and cut a cross in the centre.

Bake in a preheated oven at 190ºC (375ºF) mark 5 for 20 minutes. Leave to cool for 5 minutes, then place on the hob over a medium heat for about 5 minutes to caramelize the apples, taking care to avoid burning them. You should be able to see the brown juices bubbling through the pastry slits. Tilt the pan from time to time during cooking to distribute the juice.

Remove the tart from the heat and set aside for about 15 minutes. To remove from the tin, run a sharp knife around the inside to loosen the tart, then invert on to a plate. Serve with crème fraîche vanilla ice cream.

CREME FRAICHE VANILLA ICE CREAM

Avoid using an aluminium saucepan to heat the cream, as aluminium may cause it to curdle.

2 egg yolks
50g (2 oz) caster sugar
200ml (7 fl oz) double cream
200ml (7 fl oz) crème fraîche
1 vanilla pod
4 cloves

Beat the egg yolks and sugar together until thick and pale yellow in colour. Pour the double cream and crème fraîche into a saucepan and heat to simmering point. Meanwhile split the vanilla pod open lengthwise, using a sharp knife, then scrape out the vanilla seeds by running the knife up the open pod. Pour the cream and crème fraîche on to the egg mixture, whisking gently, then return to the saucepan and add the vanilla seeds, empty pod and cloves.

Return to the heat and cook gently, stirring constantly with a wooden spoon, until the custard thickens slightly; do not allow to boil. To test the consistency, run your finger along the back of the coated spoon. When the custard is sufficiently thickened, the finger mark will remain. Immediately remove from the heat and leave to cool.

Strain the cooled custard through a fine-meshed conical sieve. Pour into an ice cream machine and churn for about 25 minutes until thickened. If you do not have an ice cream maker, pour into a freezerproof container and and freeze until firm, removing from the freezer and beating every 45 minutes to achieve a good texture.

REGIONAL HEATS
LONDON
JO EITEL • BRUCE HYMAN • KATE WHITEMAN

KATE WHITEMAN

Kate is a food writer and translator of French manuscripts for such food gurus as Pierre Koffmann and the Roux Brothers. She works from her magnificent home in Dulwich village where, with her daughter Caroline, she breeds budgies. At last count there were eighteen.

All accomplished riders, Kate and her daughters are regularly to be found in Richmond Park exercising polo ponies. Then it's back to try out on the family one of the recipes she's just translated!

KATE WHITEMAN'S MENU

STARTER
Salad of Quail with Wild Mushrooms

MAIN COURSE
Prince of Wales Salmon (Fillets of Salmon Stuffed with Leeks)
Green Lentils with Mild Mustard Sauce
Minted Sugar Snap Peas
Steamed Broccoli
"SALMON AND MUSTARD IS TERRIFIC" LOYD

DESSERT
Ginger and Coffee Parfaits served in Brandy Snap Baskets

SALAD OF QUAIL WITH WILD MUSHROOMS

75ml (3 fl oz) olive oil
10ml (2 tsp) butter
4 quail
125g (4 oz) wild or oyster mushrooms
30ml (2 tbsp) red wine vinegar
5ml (1 tsp) Dijon mustard
30ml (2 tbsp) chopped mixed herbs
salt and freshly ground pepper
75g (3 oz) mixed salad leaves (eg frisée,
lamb's lettuce, watercress, radicchio)
4 quail's eggs

Heat 30ml (2 tbsp) oil with 5ml (1 tsp) butter in a frying pan and brown the quails all over. Transfer the quails to a roasting tin and roast in a preheated oven at 230°C (450°F) mark 8 for 15 minutes. Cover with foil and leave for 10 minutes.

Meanwhile reheat the fat remaining in the frying pan and sauté the mushrooms for 2-3 minutes. Lift out with a slotted spoon, drain and keep warm. Add the vinegar to the pan, stirring to deglaze, then pour into a bowl. Add the mustard, herbs and seasoning to taste, to make a tasty dressing.

Toss the salad leaves in 15ml (1 tbsp) dressing and arrange around the edge of 4 serving plates. Toss the mushrooms in 15ml (1 tbsp) dressing and pile in the centre. Cut off the quail legs and breasts and arrange on the salad.

Heat the remaining butter in the pan, break in the eggs and fry briefly until just cooked. Arrange on top of the mushrooms. Serve the salad while it is still warm.

PRINCE OF WALES SALMON (FILLETS OF SALMON STUFFED WITH LEEKS)

700g (1¹/2 lb) middle-cut salmon
30ml (2 tbsp) wholegrain mustard
450g (1 lb) leeks
50g (2 oz) butter
15ml (1 tbsp) tarragon leaves
salt and freshly ground pepper
15ml (1 tbsp) dry white wine

Stock:
450g (1 lb) white fish or salmon bones
and heads
1 onion
1 leek, white part only
4 button mushrooms
25g (1 oz) butter
100ml (4 fl oz) dry white wine
1 bouquet garni

First prepare the stock. Discard the gills, then chop up the fish heads and break up the fish bones; rinse well. Chop the vegetables. Heat the butter in a saucepan and sweat the vegetables until soft. Add the fish heads and bones and sweat for 3 minutes. Add the wine, bring to the boil and reduce by half. Cover the contents of the pan with cold water, add the bouquet garni and simmer, uncovered, for 30 minutes. Strain the stock into a bowl.

Meanwhile, remove the skin from the salmon and cut out the bone, leaving the fillets attached at one side. Open out like a book, tweeze out any small bones then spread with the mustard and chill while preparing the stuffing.

Thinly slice the leeks, place in a saucepan with the fish stock and cook until soft. Drain, reserving the stock. Purée the leeks in a blender or food processor with the butter and tarragon until smooth. Season to taste.

Spread half of the leek purée over the mustard-coated inside of the salmon and sandwich together. Lay the salmon on a sheet of foil, sprinkle with the wine and seal the foil. Bake in a preheated oven at 200ºC (400ºF) mark 6 for 25 minutes, then leave to rest in the foil for 5 minutes.

Mix the remaining leek purée with the fish stock to make a sauce and reheat gently. Add the cooking juices from the salmon. Cut the salmon vertically into 4 portions. Place one on each plate and pour on a little of the sauce. Serve the remaining sauce separately.

GREEN LENTILS WITH MILD MUSTARD SAUCE

125g (4 oz) green lentils
bouquet garni
salt and freshly ground pepper
125ml (4 fl oz) double cream
15-30 ml (1-2 tbsp) Dijon mustard

Place the lentils in a saucepan with the bouquet garni and 600ml (1 pint) water. Bring to the boil and boil steadily for 10 minutes, then lower the heat and simmer until tender but not mushy. Drain and add seasoning to taste.

Heat the cream with the mustard and boil for 2 minutes, then spoon over the lentils and serve.

MINTED SUGAR SNAP PEAS

175g (6 oz) sugar snap peas
1 mint sprig
salt
5ml (1 tsp) sugar

Top and tail the sugar snaps and cook with the mint in boiling salted water until cooked but still very crunchy. Refresh, drain, stir in the sugar and serve.

STEAMED BROCCOLI

200g (7 oz) broccoli
salt
25g (1 oz) butter
5ml (1 tsp) lemon juice

Divide the broccoli into florets and steam over boiling salted water until just tender. Melt the butter with the lemon juice, add to the broccoli, toss lightly and serve.

GINGER AND COFFEE PARFAIT

30ml (2 tbsp) instant coffee granules
15ml (1 tbsp) sugar
600ml (1 pint) double cream
15ml (1 tbsp) Tia Maria or other coffee
liqueur
225g (8 oz) meringues
3 pieces preserved stem ginger in syrup
15ml (1 tbsp) ginger syrup (from ginger
jar)

Dissolve the coffee and sugar in 15ml (1 tbsp) boiling water to make a syrup; cool. Whip the cream until it forms peaks, then fold in the coffee liqueur and half of the coffee syrup. Break the meringues into small pieces and fold into the cream. Finely chop the ginger and fold into the cream with the ginger syrup.

Line 4 individual moulds with cling film and fill with the parfait mixture. Drizzle the remaining coffee syrup over the top. Cover and freeze for 2 hours. Unmould and transfer to brandy snap baskets to serve.

BRANDY SNAPS BASKETS

15ml (1 tbsp) golden syrup
25g (1 oz) butter
30ml (2 tbsp) sugar
30ml (2 tbsp) flour
2.5ml (^{1}/$_2$ tsp) ground ginger
pinch of salt
2.5ml (^{1}/$_2$ tsp) brandy
2.5ml (^{1}/$_2$ tsp) lemon juice

Heat the syrup, butter and sugar gently in a saucepan until melted. Remove from the heat and stir in the remaining ingredients. Place 4 heaped spoonfuls of mixture on a baking sheet lined with non-stick paper, spacing well apart. Bake at 200°C (400°F) mark 6 for about 8 minutes, until lacy and golden.

Leave to cool for 20 seconds, then carefully lift off with a palette knife and drape over 4 small inverted greased dishes, to form baskets. Leave to harden, then carefully lift off.

REGIONAL HEATS

SCOTLAND

SUE LAWRENCE • ALASDAIR FRIEND • GORDON IRVINE

WINNER

SUE LAWRENCE

Married to Pat, a pilot with British Airways, Sue lives in the picturesque village of Crammond near Edinburgh with her three young children. Before working as a journalist, she studied French at Dundee University. She now teaches French at the local primary school.

Sue is committed to keeping fit, and attends regular aerobics classes which are interspersed with hectic games of squash. In calmer moments Sue is passionate about French art and visits exhibitions whenever she can.

SUE LAWRENCE'S MENU

STARTER
Crab tart with Aïoli

MAIN COURSE
Venison with Elderberry Jelly and Thyme
Braised Red Cabbage
Leeks with Warm Vinaigrette
Parsnip and Potato Purée
"I GO FOR THAT IN A BIG WAY" SUE MacGREGOR

DESSERT
Lemon Curd Ice Cream with Bramble Coulis
Petticoat Tail Shortbread
"IT'S THE SORT OF SHORTBREAD THAT WOULDN'T STAY LONG IN THE TIN AT MY HOUSE" SUE MacGREGOR

CRAB TART WITH AÏOLI

Shortcrust Pastry:
225g (8 oz) plain flour
1.25ml ($^1/_4$ tsp) salt
grated rind of 1 orange
125g (4 oz) unsalted butter
1 egg yolk

Filling:
350g (12 oz) cooked crabmeat (mixture of white and brown meat)
3 eggs, beaten
10ml (2 tsp) lemon juice
pinch of cayenne pepper
salt
125ml (4 fl oz) double cream

Aïoli:
2 cloves garlic
1 egg
15ml (1 tbsp) lemon juice (approximately)
125-150ml (4-5 fl oz) sunflower oil
50-75ml (2-3 fl oz) olive oil

To Garnish:
chervil sprigs

To make the pastry, sift the flour and salt together. Place in a food processor and add the grated orange rind. Add the butter in pieces and process briefly until the mixture resembles fine breadcrumbs. Add the egg yolk and process for a few seconds until the dough holds together in a ball. Wrap in cling film and leave to rest in the refrigerator for 30 minutes.

Roll out the pastry on a lightly floured surface and use to line a 23cm (9 inch) flan tin. Leave to rest in the refrigerator for 20 minutes, then prick the base with a fork. Bake blind in a preheated oven at 190°C (375°F) mark 5 for 10 minutes.

For the filling, mix together the crabmeat, eggs, lemon juice, cayenne and salt, then stir in the cream. Spoon the filling into the pastry case and bake for 25-35 minutes.

To prepare the aïoli, crush the garlic with a little salt. Put into a food processor or blender, add the egg and process for 30 seconds, then add the lemon juice and process for 10 seconds. With the machine running, slowly pour in the oils through the feeder tube until the aïoli reaches the consistency of mayonnaise. Taste and add salt and extra lemon juice if required.

Serve the crab tart warm with the aïoli. Garnish with chervil.

VENISON WITH ELDERBERRY JELLY AND THYME

Use farmed, well- hung venison for this dish.

2 venison fillets, each about 350g (12 oz), trimmed
30ml (2 tbsp) hazelnut oil (approximately)
small handful of thyme sprigs
15ml (1 tbsp) olive oil
50g (2 oz) butter
2 glasses (good) red wine
450ml (3/4 pint) venison stock
30ml (2 tbsp) elderberry jelly
salt and freshly ground pepper

To Garnish:
few elderberries (fresh or frozen)
thyme sprigs

Brush the venison fillets with hazelnut oil and press thyme sprigs all over them. Cover and leave to marinate for 1-2 hours.

Heat the olive oil and half of the butter in a frying pan, then add the venison. Cook, turning, for about 6 minutes until sealed and browned on all sides.

Transfer to an ovenproof dish and leave to rest in a preheated oven at 150°C (300°F) mark 2 for no longer than 8 minutes.

Meanwhile, add the wine to the frying pan, stirring to deglaze, then reduce to about half of the volume. Add the stock and reduce by about half. Add a few thyme sprigs with the elderberry jelly. Stir well and reduce slightly. Add the remaining butter, in pieces, to give a glossy finish. Check the seasoning. Strain the sauce into a jug.

To serve, cut the venison into 1cm (1/2 inch) medallions. Arrange in an overlapping circle on each plate, with the braised red cabbage in the centre. Spoon the sauce around the meat. Garnish with thyme and elderberries.

BRAISED RED CABBAGE

10ml (2 tsp) olive oil
15g (1/2 oz) butter
50g (2 oz) unsmoked bacon, derinded and
chopped
1 onion, chopped
2 cloves garlic, crushed
450g (1 lb) red cabbage, sliced
1 cooking apple
300ml (1/2 pint) mixed red wine and stock
pinch of cloves
freshly grated nutmeg
1.25ml (1/4 tsp) salt
freshly ground pepper

Heat the oil and butter in a large pan and sauté the bacon, onion and garlic until softened. Add the red cabbage and cook, stirring, for 10 minutes.

Peel, core and chop the apple. Add to the cabbage with the remaining ingredients and bring to the boil.

Transfer to an ovenproof dish, cover and cook in a preheated oven at 160°C (325°F) mark 3 for 2-3 hours.

LEEKS WITH WARM VINAIGRETTE

4 medium leeks

Vinaigrette:
5ml (1 tsp) Dijon mustard
15ml (1 tbsp) blueberry vinegar
coarse sea salt
freshly ground pepper
45-75ml (3-5 tbsp) olive oil

Cut the leeks diagonally into slices and steam over boiling water for 2 minutes, until cooked but still crunchy. Drain.

For the vinaigrette, mix together the mustard, vinegar and seasoning to taste. Whisk in enough olive oil to give a thick emulsion.

Toss the leeks in the vinaigrette and serve immediately.

PARSNIP AND POTATO PURÉE

For the crumb topping, I use Italian bread, which gives a delicious crunchy texture.

600g (1¹/₄ lb) parsnips
350g (12 oz) potatoes
salt
40g (1¹/₂ oz) butter
125ml (4 fl oz) double cream
pinch of freshly grated nutmeg
coarse sea salt
freshly ground pepper

Topping:
50g (2 oz) fresh white breadcrumbs
a little olive oil and butter
handful of thyme leaves

Cook the parsnips and potatoes in boiling salted water until just tender; drain. Pass through a mouli-legume or mash to a smooth purée, using a potato masher.

Gently heat the butter, cream, nutmeg and seasoning in a large pan. Add the vegetables and heat through, stirring.

For the topping, fry the bread-crumbs in a little olive oil and melted butter, with the thyme leaves, until crisp. Sprinkle over the parsnip and potato purée to serve.

PETTICOAT TAIL SHORTBREAD

This is a traditional Scottish shortbread, which you can of course serve as a tea-time treat. I particularly like to serve it as a complement to lemon curd ice cream with bramble coulis.

175g (6 oz) slightly salted butter
50g (2 oz) caster sugar
175g (6 oz) plain flour, sifted
50g (2 oz) farola (fine semolina)
caster sugar for sprinkling

Cream the butter and sugar together in a bowl until light and fluffy. Sift the flour and farola (semolina) together, add to the creamed mixture and knead briefly to a smooth dough. Divide into 3 equal pieces and lightly press each one in a 15cm (6 inch) fluted sandwich tin. Prick all over with a fork. Bake in a preheated oven at 150°C (300°F) mark 2 for 35-45 minutes until golden.

Mark the shortbread into wedges while it is still hot. Allow to cool. Sprinkle with sugar to serve.

LEMON CURD ICE CREAM WITH BRAMBLE COULIS

Homemade lemon curd is essential for this ice cream: no bought product is good enough! I have included a recipe here, but if you have some homemade lemon curd to hand, you will need 350g (12 oz).

Lemon Curd:
3 eggs
grated rind of 3 large lemons
170ml (6 fl oz) freshly squeezed lemon juice
125g (4 oz) unsalted butter
225g (8 oz) granulated sugar

Ice Cream:
500ml (16 fl oz) natural yogurt (not the set variety)

Bramble Coulis:
350g (12 oz) blackberries
50-75g (2-3 oz) icing sugar
juice of 1/2 lemon
10ml (2 tsp) framboise eau-de-vie

To Decorate:
blackberries
mint sprigs

To make the lemon curd, beat the eggs lightly, then mix in the lemon rind and juice, butter in pieces, and the sugar. Place in the top of a double boiler or in a heatproof bowl over a pan of simmering water. Heat gently, stirring frequently, until the sugar has dissolved and the mixture has thickened; about 20 minutes. Cool, then store in a sterilised jar until required.

To make the ice cream, gradually stir 350g (12 oz) lemon curd into the yogurt until evenly mixed. Pour into a freezerproof container and freeze until firm.

For the bramble coulis, place all the ingredients in a food processor or blender and work until smooth. Pass through a sieve to remove pips, then chill.

To serve, scoop the ice cream on to individual plates. Pour the bramble coulis around the lemon ice cream and decorate with blackberries and mint sprigs. Serve with petticoat tail shortbread.

REGIONAL HEATS
SCOTLAND
SUE LAWRENCE • ALASDAIR FRIEND • GORDON IRVINE

ALASDAIR FRIEND

L iving in Edinburgh, Alasdair is a freelance journalist writing mainly lifestyle pieces for The Scotsman and Scotland on Sunday.

He is a fanatical skier and practices enthusiastically on the Hillend dry slope - the largest in the country.

Recently Alasdair has taken up the unusual sport of husky racing, which has developed from an article he wrote on the subject. Standing astride a primitive chariot-like tricycle, teams of huskies rush him through the countryside at alarming speed. Ready when you are, Mr de Mille!

ALASDAIR FRIEND'S MENU

STARTER
Wild Mushroom Eggs

MAIN COURSE
Leeks with Feta Cheese and Thyme en Croûte
'Burnt' Aubergine and Mint Sauce
'Floddies' (Parsnip and Potato Pancakes)
"THAT SAUCE IS A TRIUMPH" SUE MACGREGOR

DESSERT
Milk and Carrageen Puddings with Jasmine and Cardamom
"IT WOBBLES IN ALL THE RIGHT PLACES" LOYD
"THE CARDAMOM IS THE TOUCH OF GENIUS" SUE MACGREGOR

WILD MUSHROOM EGGS

handful of dried ceps or other dried wild mushrooms
25g (1 oz) butter
200g (7 oz) cultivated mushrooms
300ml (1/2 pint) double cream
squeeze of lemon juice
salt and freshly ground black pepper
1 clove garlic, crushed
4 free-range eggs

To Serve:
salad leaves

Rinse the dried mushrooms carefully, then soak in sufficient warm water to just cover them for 30 minutes. Melt the butter in a pan, add the cultivated mushrooms and fry gently until softened. Stir in the cream and wild mushrooms with their soaking liquid. Add the lemon juice, seasoning and garlic and simmer until the liquid has reduced. Transfer to a food processor or blender and purée until smooth. Keep the sauce warm.

Break each egg into a well buttered mould. Place in a bain marie, or baking tin containing enough boiling water to come halfway up the sides of the moulds. Cover, leaving a little gap for the steam to escape, and bake in a preheated oven at 190°C (375°F) mark 5 for 5-6 minutes or until cooked to your liking.

Carefully remove the baked eggs from their moulds and place on warmed serving plates. Surround with the mushroom sauce and garnish with salad leaves to serve.

LEEKS WITH FETA CHEESE AND THYME EN CROUTE

For this dish, you will need *zahtar*, a Middle Eastern condiment—of thyme, sesame seeds and lemon juice—available from specialist shops and delicatessens. Make sure you use feta prepared from cow's milk, as it has a superior flavour.

4 large leeks
salt
450g (1 lb) packet puff pastry
zahtar to taste (see above)
extra virgin olive oil for sprinkling
400g (14 oz) feta cheese, crumbled
beaten egg to glaze

Trim the leeks to 10cm (4 inch) lengths. Place in a pan of boiling salted water, remove from the heat and let stand for 5 minutes. Drain the leeks thoroughly and set aside.

Meanwhile roll out the puff pastry on a lightly floured surface. Cut out four 12 x 7.5cm (5 x 3 inch) sheets and four slightly larger sheets. Spread a line of zahtar along the middle of each of the smaller pastry sheets, then sprinkle a line of olive oil on top. Cover with a line of feta cheese.

Halve the leeks lengthwise, without cutting right through, then open out and dampen the centres with a sprinkling of water. Place cut-side down on the line of feta. Brush the edges of the pastry with beaten egg and position the larger pastry squares on top. Press the edges together to seal, trim and decorate with shapes cut from the pastry trimmings. Brush with egg to glaze. Bake in a preheated oven at 200°C (400°F) mark 6 for 25-30 minutes until golden brown.

Serve immediately, with 'burnt' aubergine and mint sauce, and the 'floddies'.

'BURNT' AUBERGINE AND MINT SAUCE

2 medium aubergines
salt
oil for deep frying
500ml (16 fl oz) Greek yogurt
juice of 1 lemon
1 clove garlic
mint sprigs to garnish

Peel the aubergines and cut the flesh into cubes. Sprinkle with salt and leave to degorge for 15 minutes. Rinse and pat dry with kitchen paper.

Heat the oil in a deep fryer. When it is very hot, add the aubergine cubes and fry until golden brown. Remove and drain on kitchen paper, then place in a food processor or blender. Add the remaining ingredients and work to a smooth sauce. Cool before serving, garnished with mint sprigs.

'FLODDIES' (PARSNIP AND POTATO PANCAKES)

3 large potatoes
2 parsnips
oil for shallow frying
salt

Finely shred the potatoes and parsnips, using the finest shredding blade of a food processor. Immediately transfer to a bowl of cold water.

Heat the oil in a large frying pan and position metal rings or pastry cutters in the oil. Drain the potatoes and pat dry with kitchen paper. When the oil is hot, fill each metal ring with shredded potato and parsnip. Cook until the underside is golden brown, then turn and cook the other side. Drain on kitchen paper and serve the pancakes piping hot.

MILK AND CARRAGEEN PUDDINGS WITH JASMINE AND CARDAMOM

Carrageen is a reddish coloured seaweed which is found on beaches around Britain. It is also available dried, from healthfood shops.

handful of carrageen (fresh or dried)
1.2 litres (2 pints) milk
20 green cardamom pods
handful of dried jasmine flowers
15-30ml (2-3 tbsp) sugar
juice of 2 oranges
250ml (8 fl oz) water
45ml (3 tbsp) honey
handful of dried hibiscus flowers

To Decorate:
fresh jasmine leaves and flowers

Rinse the carrageen leaves in warm water to clean thoroughly and remove salt. Put the milk in a saucepan and add the carrageen. Open the cardamom pods, extract the seeds and crush them with a rolling pin. Add to the milk, with the jasmine flowers and sugar to taste. Bring to the boil and simmer for about 10 minutes until the milk appears to thicken.

Strain the milk through a fine-meshed sieve into ramekins or individual moulds. Leave in the refrigerator to set.

To make the sauce, put the orange juice, water and honey in a saucepan and heat gently until evenly blended, then add the hibiscus flowers and simmer until reduced by about half. Allow to cool, then strain.

Turn out the puddings on to individual plates. Spoon on the sauce and decorate with fresh jasmine to serve.

REGIONAL HEATS

SCOTLAND

SUE LAWRENCE • ALASDAIR FRIEND • GORDON IRVINE

GORDON IRVINE

A senior engineer at Yarrow Shipbuilders, Glasgow, where Royal Navy ships are constructed, Gordon says that most of his day is spent at a computer. No wonder he likes to get into the hills in the beautiful surrounding countryside for some serious walking with his wife, Liz. Her family have a farm locally where Gordon often lends a hand, and he rarely misses his Tuesday night five-a-side football match.

At work his group of friends are all devoted cooks, and a great deal of the lunch hour is spent discussing last night's supper, or next week's dinner party. All very French, but with Scots accents!

GORDON IRVINE'S MENU

STARTER
Oysters and Scallops in Cream Sauce with Parmesan
"THE TENDEREST SCALLOP I'VE EVER TASTED" SUE MACGREGOR

MAIN COURSE
Gaelic Steak
New Potatoes
Sautéed Morels
Carrots flavoured with Orange

DESSERT
Hazelnut Praline Ice Cream served with a Chocolate Sauce
"NICELY UNSWEET CHOCOLATE SAUCE" LOYD

OYSTERS AND SCALLOPS IN CREAM SAUCE WITH PARMESAN

12 oysters
6 scallops
150ml (¹/4 pint) double cream
salt and freshly ground pepper
freshly grated Parmesan cheese for
sprinkling

Prise open the oyster and scallop shells over a bowl to collect the liquid. Pass the liquid through a fine-meshed conical sieve to remove any grit and place in a saucepan. Bring to the boil and simmer until reduced by about two thirds.

Halve the white scallop meat, discarding the coral. Add to the pan with the oysters. As soon as the liquid begins to bubble, remove the oysters and scallops with a slotted spoon and wrap in a warm, damp towel.

Add the cream to the liquid. Bring to the boil and cook, stirring, until the sauce is thick enough to coat the back of the spoon. Check the seasoning.

Divide the oysters and scallop pieces between individual gratin dishes. Spoon over the sauce and sprinkle lightly with Parmesan. Place under a preheated hot grill until the topping is lightly browned. Serve immediately.

GAELIC STEAK

If you prefer, buy 4 individual fillet steaks, rather than a whole piece, and simply fry on both sides until cooked to your liking. Serve each steak on a bed of haggis.

1 kg (2 lb) fillet steak, in 1 piece
1 haggis
40g (1¹/2 oz) butter
30ml (2 tbsp) olive oil
3 shallots, finely chopped
2 garlic cloves, chopped
250ml (8 fl oz) demi glace
salt and freshly ground pepper
30ml (2 tbsp) whisky

Trim the steak if necessary. Skin the haggis, then cut into slices about 1cm (¹/2 inch) thick, and dot with a third of the butter. Place in an ovenproof dish. Cover with foil and cook in a preheated oven at 220°C (425°F) mark 7 for 30 minutes, turning the slices from time to time.

Heat the oil and remaining butter in a frying pan, add the meat and brown all over. Transfer to a roasting tin and roast in the oven for 30 minutes, or longer if you prefer.

Add the shallots to the frying pan and cook for 2 minutes. Add the garlic and cook for 1 minute. Stir in the demi glace. Bring to the boil and check the seasoning. Just before serving, add the whisky.

Arrange a bed out of haggis on each plate. Slice the beef thickly, allowing 3 pieces per person, and place on top of the haggis. Spoon over the sauce.

Serve with morels sautéed in butter, carrots cooked in orange juice, and new potatoes.

Note: A recipe for demi glace is given on page 49.

HAZELNUT PRALINE ICE CREAM

Praline:
25g (1 oz) caster sugar
25g (1 oz) hazelnuts, toasted and skinned

Ice Cream:
6 egg yolks
140g (4¹/2 oz) caster sugar
475ml (17¹/2 fl oz) milk
5ml (1 tsp) instant coffee powder
90ml (3 fl oz) extra thick double cream

To make the praline, gently heat the sugar in a small pan until completely dissolved and golden in colour. Add the hazelnuts and cook for 30 seconds, taking care that the sugar does not burn. Pour the mixture on to a plate and leave until cold and hard. Place the praline between 2 sheets of greaseproof paper and crush with a rolling pin.

For the ice cream, whisk the egg yolks and 40g (1¹/2 oz) sugar together until pale and thick enough to leave a ribbon, when the whisk is lifted. Put the milk and remaining sugar in a saucepan and heat gently until the sugar is dissolved, then bring to the boil. Pour the boiling milk on to the egg mixture, whisking continuously until the sauce is thick enough to coat the back of a spoon. Pass the sauce through a fine-meshed conical sieve into a bowl and place a piece of greaseproof paper on top to prevent a skin forming. Allow to cool.

Add the coffee powder to the cooled custard, then stir in the cream and praline. Transfer the mixture to an ice cream machine and churn until thick. If you do not have an ice cream maker, pour into a freezerproof container and freeze until firm. Remove from the freezer and whisk occasionally, every 20-30 minutes, during freezing to improve the texture of the ice cream.

Serve the hazelnut praline ice cream with hot or cold chocolate sauce.

CHOCOLATE SAUCE

150g (5 oz) plain chocolate
170ml (6 fl oz) double cream
25g (1 oz) butter

Melt the chocolate in a bain marie or heatproof bowl over a saucepan of simmering water.

Put the cream in a saucepan over a low heat and bring to a simmer, whisking gently. Pour on to the melted chocolate, stirring constantly. Pour the mixture back into the saucepan and let simmer for 10 seconds. Remove from the heat and beat in the butter, a little at a time. Serve the chocolate sauce hot or cold.

REGIONAL HEATS

THE NORTH

SARAH BEATTIE • JEAN HAYTON • LOUISE SOLDEN

WINNER

SARAH BEATTIE

O ne of the first vegetarian cooks to qualify for the finals of *MasterChef*, Sarah, from Pickering in North Yorkshire, hopes soon to spread the message with her book "Neither Fish nor Fowl: The Green Gourmand."

Currently in the midst of restoring their period cottage, Sarah and Michael, a freelance writer, together with their three children, generally find their weekly way to the local auction in search of bargain antiques for their home.

SARAH BEATTIE'S MENU

STARTER
Ravioli in Brodo di Aranci
"I'M VERY KEEN ON THAT" LOYD

MAIN COURSE
Cornucopia of Wild Mushrooms and Chestnuts in Madeira
Spring Cabbage with Mustard Seeds
Celeriac Bâtons
"OH, THAT IS MAGNIFICENT" KEN LIVINGSTON

DESSERT
Blackbottom Cheesecake with Strawberries

RAVIOLI IN BRODO DI ARANCI

The quantity of pasta dough given here is more than sufficient for the ravioli; it isn't practical to make a smaller amount. Use the extra pasta for lasagne sheets.

Ravioli Filling:
a little olive oil
1 clove garlic, chopped
1 small head fennel, chopped
50g (2 oz) ricotta cheese
freshly ground black pepper

Pasta Dough:
225g (8 oz) strong plain flour
2.5ml (¹/₂ tsp) salt
2 eggs

Broth:
25g (1 oz) butter or margarine
1kg (2 lb) carrots, grated
1 large Spanish onion, finely chopped
2.5cm (1 inch) piece fresh root ginger, grated
1.2 litres (2 pints) vegetable stock
juice of 4 sweet oranges
pinch of brown sugar

To Garnish:
orange zest
fennel leaves

To make the ravioli filling, heat the oil in a pan, add the garlic and fennel, cover and sweat the vegetables over a low heat until meltingly soft. Stir in the ricotta. Season with plenty of pepper. Set aside.

To make the pasta dough, sift the flour and salt into a bowl, then work in the eggs. Bind the dough with a little water, about 15-30ml (1-2 tbsp), then knead well. Work until smooth and elastic. Put the dough through pasta rollers until very thin and silky, or roll out as thinly as possible.

Using a 5cm (2 inch) cutter, stamp out rounds. Place a teaspoonful of filling on the centre of each one. Dampen the edges, fold over the filling and press the edges together to seal. Leave on a wire rack to dry, while making the broth.

For the broth, melt the butter or margarine in a large pan, add the carrots, onion and ginger and cook gently for 5 minutes. Add the stock and simmer for 20 minutes.

Pass the broth through a fine-meshed conical sieve into a clean pan. Add the orange juice and brown sugar. Season with salt and plenty of black pepper to taste. Reheat gently until barely simmering. Poach the ravioli in the broth for 3-5 minutes.

Ladle into warmed soup plates and garnish with orange zest and fennel leaves to serve.

CORNUCOPIA OF WILD MUSHROOMS AND CHESTNUTS IN MADEIRA

For this dish, use pied de mouton mushrooms if you can find them. Otherwise, use a mixture of oyster and brown cap mushrooms.

Pastry:
225g (8 oz) plain flour
pinch of salt
50g (2 oz) sunflower spread
50g (2 oz) butter

Filling:
25g (1 oz) butter
3 cloves garlic, finely chopped
225g (8 oz) shallots, finely chopped
350g (12 oz) mushrooms, chopped
50g (2 oz) stoned prunes, chopped
25g (1 oz) dried chestnuts, reconstituted (see note) and chopped
few sage leaves, chopped
1/4 bottle Madeira

To Glaze:
1 egg yolk, mixed with a little water

To make the pastry, sift the flour and salt into a bowl and rub in the fat until the mixture resembles breadcrumbs. Bind with a little water. Wrap the pastry in cling film and leave to rest in the refrigerator.

For the filling, heat the butter in a pan, add the garlic and shallots and cook gently until softened. Add the mushrooms to the pan and cook for 5 minutes. Add the prunes, chestnuts and sage, cook for a few minutes, then add the Madeira. Remove from the heat and allow to stand for an hour if possible.

Roll out the pastry and cut into 1cm (1/2 inch) strips, then wind around cream horn tins, overlapping the strips. Brush with egg glaze and bake in a preheated oven at 190ºC (375ºF) mark 5 for 20 minutes. Bring the mushroom filling to a simmer, stirring occasionally, and reduce slightly.

Remove the pastry horns from their moulds and spoon in the mushroom filling. Arrange on individual plates with plenty of the filling spilling out of the horns.

Note: I have found that the best way to reconstitute dried chestnuts is to cover them with water and cook gently in a low oven for about 1 hour.

SPRING CABBAGE WITH MUSTARD SEEDS

This is a delicious way of cooking cabbage. It retains bite and colour — and the mustard seeds impart a wonderful flavour.

450g (1 lb) spring cabbage
15g (1/2 oz) butter
2.5-5ml (1/2-1 tsp) black mustard seeds
salt and freshly ground pepper

Quarter the cabbage, discarding the core, and cut into 5mm (1/4 inch) strips across the leaves. Heat the butter in a heavy-based pan and add the mustard seeds. Cover the pan tightly and cook, shaking the pan occasionally, until the mustard seeds pop. Add the cabbage, cover and cook over a moderate heat, shaking frequently, for 2-3 minutes. Check the seasoning and serve immediately.

CELERIAC BATONS

1 large celeriac
25g (1oz) butter
freshly ground black pepper

Simply peel the celeriac and cut into even bâtons, about 4cm (1¹/₂ inches) long and a little less than 1cm (¹/₂ inch) thick. Heat the butter in a heavy-based pan, add the celeriac bâtons with plenty of black pepper. Cook, covered, over a low heat, shaking the pan occasionally, for 15-20 minutes until the celeriac is tender.

BLACKBOTTOM CHEESECAKE WITH STRAWBERRIES

This creamy exotic dessert has a very dark, sticky, fudgy chocolate base and a passion fruit flavoured cheesecake layer. Topped with 'flowers' of deep red fragrant strawberries and set off with a crescent of strawberry purée, it is irresistible. A guest at my house once proposed to this ultimate chocolate confection!

Base:
50g (2oz) dark chocolate (see note)
50g (2oz) golden granulated sugar
15ml (1 tbsp) strong black
(espresso) coffee
dash of dark rum
50g (2oz) unsalted butter
1 large free-range egg

Filling:
125ml (4oz) cream cheese
150ml (¹/₄ pint) soured cream
2 passion fruit
150ml (¹/₄ pint) double cream

To Finish:
250g (8oz) ripe fragrant strawberries

Break up the chocolate and place in a bowl over a pan of hot water, with the sugar, coffee and rum. Warm, stirring, until the chocolate has melted. Remove from the heat. Using a large whisk, beat in the butter in small pieces, a little at a time, until evenly blended. Whisk in the egg.

Butter the insides of 4 crumpet rings and stand them on a baking tray lined with non-stick baking parchment. Divide the chocolate mixture evenly between the rings and bake in a preheated oven at 150°C (300°F) mark 2 for approximately 40 minutes. Allow to cool, then chill.

Meanwhile make the filling. Beat the cream cheese and soured cream together in a bowl. Halve the passion fruit and scoop out the pulp and seeds into a sieve over the bowl. Press the fruit through the sieve on to the cream cheese mixture, then beat in. Add the double cream and whip until the mixture is quite stiff.

Unmold the chocolate bases on to individual serving plates. Cover with an even thick layer of filling. Arrange overlapping strawberry slices on top, with their pointed ends radiating out like flower petals. Purée the remaining strawberries in a blender or food processor, then sieve to remove pips. Spoon a crescent of strawberry purée on to each plate beside the cheesecake, and pipe fine lines of cream cheese filling across it to decorate. Serve immediately.

Note: For the base, make sure you use a quality chocolate containing at least 47% cocoa solids, but preferably 60% for optimum flavour.

REGIONAL HEATS

THE NORTH

SARAH BEATTIE • JEAN HAYTON • LOUISE SOLDEN

JEAN HAYTON

When we visited Jean on her husband's family farm near Harrogate, she was busy with the lambs and calves. She now has a part-time job, preparing lunch for the mentally ill at the nearby day centre.

Learning to relax is important to Jean, and she has recently taken a course in aromatherapy. Whether garage proprietor husband David, or their two children, will let her practise on them is not known. Upholstery is Jean's other form of relaxation, which she is currently putting to good use by restoring a set of antique dining chairs.

JEAN HAYTON'S MENU

STARTER

Smoked Salmon Trout Roulade with Apple and Horseradish Cream, and Watercress Salad

MAIN COURSE

Noisettes of Venison with Wild Mushrooms and Marc-de-Champagne Sauce
Tartlets of Caramelised Apple
Braised Carrots and Parsnips with Toasted Pine Nuts
Spinach Darioles with Garlic
Rosti Potatoes

DESSERT

Citrus Flans with Caramelized Oranges and Chantilly Cream
"WONDERFUL PASTRY" VALENTINA HARRIS
"A GREAT UNANIMOUS MMMM FROM ALL OF US" LOYD

SMOKED SALMON TROUT ROULADE WITH APPLE AND HORSERADISH CREAM AND WATERCRESS SALAD

Delicate pink smoked salmon trout has a fine flavour. It is sold freshly sliced or vacuum-packed, like smoked salmon.

Roulade:

125g (4 oz) smoked salmon trout fillets
1 small bunch of dill sprigs
150ml (5 fl oz) fromage frais
5ml (1 tsp) lime juice
pinch of paprika

Apple and Horseradish Cream:

1 small cooking apple, peeled,cored and sliced
30ml (2 tbsp) water
1 knob of unsalted butter
90ml (3 fl oz) fromage frais
2.5ml (1/2 tsp) grated fresh horseradish (or creamed horseradish)
5ml (1 tsp) lime juice
pinch of sugar
salt and freshly ground black pepper

Watercress Salad:

2 bunches watercress
1 large orange
15g (1/2 oz) walnuts, roughly chopped

Dressing:

30ml (2 tbsp) walnut oil
15ml (1 tbsp) red wine vinegar
salt and freshly ground pepper

To make the roulade, lay a 20 x 30cm (8 x 12 inch) piece of foil on your work surface. Arrange the trout fillets, top to tail and overlapping slightly, in a rectangle on the foil. Place another sheet of foil on top and press with a rolling pin to flatten the trout. Remove the top sheet of the foil.

Set aside a few dill fonds for garnish; finely chop the rest and stir into the fromage frais with the lime juice and paprika. Spread the mixture evenly over the trout.

Carefully roll up the roulade as tightly as possible from a long side, using the foil to help you. Tweeze out any small bones from the trout as you roll. Wrap the roulade tightly in foil and chill in the refrigerator.

To make the apple and horseradish cream, put the apple slices in a pan with the water and butter. Cook until very soft and pulpy. Allow to cool. Stir in the fromage frais, grated horseradish, lime juice, sugar and seasoning to taste. Chill.

To prepare the salad, remove any tough stalks and leaves from the watercress, then place in a bowl. Peel and segment the orange over a small pan to collect the juice. Add the orange segments to the watercress with the chopped walnuts.

For the dressing, whisk the walnut oil and red wine vinegar into the orange juice. Season liberally with salt and pepper. Warm over a low heat for 2-3 minutes.

To serve, unwrap the roulade and cut into 1cm (1/2 inch) slices. Place a portion on each serving plate. Add a spoonful of apple and horseradish cream, dust with paprika and garnish with dill. Pour the warm dressing over the salad, toss to coat and arrange a little on each plate. Serve immediately.

NOISETTES OF VENISON WITH WILD MUSHROOMS AND MARC-DE-CHAMPAGNE SAUCE

1kg (2 lb) boned saddle of venison, bones reserved
1 onion, chopped
1 carrot, chopped
1 clove garlic
1.5 litres (2¹/2 pints) water
1 bouquet garni (piece of celery, parsley, thyme and sage)
25g (1 oz) flour
250ml (8 fl oz) Bordeaux Blanc or similar white wine
15ml (1 tbsp) rowan jelly
salt and freshly ground black pepper
50g (2 oz) butter
125g (4 oz) wild mushrooms
60ml (2 fl oz) Marc-de-Champagne

Marinade:
125ml (4 fl oz) grapeseed oil
handful of thyme leaves
6 juniper berries, crushed

For the marinade, mix the grapeseed oil, thyme and juniper berries in a shallow dish. Cut the saddle of venison into 12 noisettes, add to the dish and leave to marinate in a cool place.

Place the veal bones in a roasting tin and roast in a preheated hot oven until browned all over. Put the vegetables, garlic, water and bouquet garni in a large pan. Add the veal bones and bring to a simmer. Sprinkle the juices in the roasting pan with the flour and cook, stirring, until lightly browned. Whisk in the white wine. Continue to cook until the mixture thickens, then add to the stock pan. Simmer for 2¹/2 hours, then strain into a clean pan, and reduce by half. Stir in the rowan jelly and seasoning.

Heat a large sauté pan or frying pan and sear the noisettes of venison on both sides to seal; the oil from the marinade will prevent them from sticking. Lower the heat and cook for 3 minutes on each side. Keep warm in a cool oven while you finish the sauce.

Heat half of the butter in the pan and quickly sauté the mushrooms until tender; remove with a slotted spoon. Deglaze the pan with the Marc-de-Champagne. Add the sautéed mushrooms, swirl in the remaining butter and adjust the seasoning.

To serve, spoon enough sauce on to each warmed serving plate to cover the base and position 3 noisettes of venison to one side. Position a dariole of spinach and a tartlet of caramelised apples on each plate. Serve the rosti potatoes and braised carrots and parsnips separately.

TARTLETS OF CARAMELISED APPLE

For these tartlets, use the leftover pastry from the orange tart (see page 82).

50g (2 oz) pastry
1 large cooking apple
15ml (1 tbsp) lemon juice
25g (1 oz) butter
25g (1 oz) sugar

Line 4 tiny individual tartlet tins with pastry. Prick the bases with a fork and bake blind in a preheated oven at 200°C (400°F) mark 6 for 5-10 minutes. Peel and core the apple and cut into fairly thick slices, so that they do not break up during cooking; toss in lemon juice.

Heat the butter and sugar in a heavy-based pan until the mixture begins to caramelise. Add the apple slices and toss briefly, to coat. Arrange 2 apple slices in each tartlet case and serve warm.

SUE LAWRENCE'S MAIN COURSE (REGIONAL HEAT)

Venison with Elderberry Jelly and Thyme
Braised Red Cabbage
Leeks with Warm Vinaigrette
Parsnip and Potato Purée

SARAH BEATTIE'S MAIN COURSE (REGIONAL HEAT)

Cornucopia of Wild Mushrooms and Chestnuts in Madeira
Spring Cabbage with Mustard Seeds
Celeriac Bâtons

BRAISED CARROTS AND PARSNIPS WITH TOASTED PINE NUTS

450g (1 lb) carrots, cut into julienne
50g (2 oz) butter
350g (12 oz) parsnips, cut into julienne
salt and freshly ground black pepper
25g (1 oz) pine nuts, toasted

Put the carrots in a pan with the butter and just enough water to cover. Boil quickly to evaporate the water, turning the carrots to coat with the butter. Add the parsnips and toss to coat. Transfer to an ovenproof dish and season with salt and pepper. Cook in the top of a preheated oven at 200°C (400°F) mark 6 for 20 minutes until lightly caramelised, turning the vegetables from time to time. Sprinkle with pine nuts to serve.

SPINACH DARIOLES WITH GARLIC

450g (1 lb) spinach
25g (1 oz) butter
1 clove garlic, finely chopped
a little double cream to bind
julienne of lightly cooked carrot to garnish

Remove any tough stalks from the spinach leaves and blanch in boiling water; drain. Pick out some well-shaped leaves and use them to line 4 buttered dariole moulds or ramekins, leaving enough overhanging the sides to cover the top.

Drain the rest of the spinach thoroughly in a colander, pressing to extract as much moisture as possible. Chop finely. Heat the butter in a pan and sauté the garlic gently for 1 minute. Add the spinach and warm through. Bind with a little double cream and spoon into the dariole moulds.

Press the outer leaves over the top to cover and place in a large pan. Add sufficient water to come halfway up the sides of the moulds and carefully simmer for 10-15 minutes.

To serve, unmould the spinach on to warmed plates and garnish with carrot julienne.

ROSTI POTATOES

1kg (2 lb) potatoes
50-75g (2-3 oz) unsalted butter
5ml (1tsp) salt
freshly ground black pepper

Boil the potatoes for 7 minutes until barely tender. Drain and leave until cold. Skin the potatoes and grate coarsely. Melt the butter in a sauté pan. Using a 7.5cm (3 inch) plain cutter, shape small rounds of grated potato. Transfer to the pan and season with salt and pepper. Fry over a moderate heat for 8 minutes, pressing the rosti with a spatula. Turn and cook the other side until golden brown. Keep warm in the oven, while cooking the remainder.

CITRUS FLANS WITH CARAMELISED ORANGES AND CHANTILLY CREAM

Pastry:
300g (10 oz) plain flour
2.5ml (¹/2 tsp) salt
200ml (7 oz) butter (at room temperature)
2 egg yolks
15-45ml (1-3 tbsp) water

Filling:
4 eggs
175g (6 oz) sugar
150ml (¹/4 pint) freshly squeezed lemon juice
120ml (4 fl oz) freshly squeezed orange juice
50g (2 oz) butter
60ml (4 tbsp) double cream

To Decorate:
2 oranges
icing sugar to glaze
75g (3 oz) flaked almonds, toasted

To make the pastry, sift the flour and salt onto a work surface. Make a well in the centre and put in the butter pieces, with the egg yolks. Using one hand, work the butter and yolks together, gradually drawing in the flour until it is all incorporated. Add as much of the water as you need to give a soft pliable, but not sticky, dough.

Roll out the dough and use to line four 10-12cm (4-5 inch) individual loose-bottomed fluted flan tins. Line with greaseproof paper and fill with baking beans. Bake blind in a preheated oven at 200°C (400°F) mark 6 for 5-10 minutes. Remove paper and beans and return the flans to the oven for 3-5 minutes, until golden and crisp. Leave in their tins on a wire rack to cool.

To make the filling, put the eggs, sugar, lemon and orange juices in a bowl and beat well. Place over a pan of simmering water and whisk continuously until thickened.

Melt the butter with the cream in a pan over a low heat, then blend into the orange mixture. Cook for a further 2 minutes. Pour into the cooked flan cases and leave to cool slightly.

Meanwhile, peel and segment the oranges, removing all pith. Liberally cover with icing sugar and place under a preheated hot grill until caramelised.

To serve, sprinkle toasted almonds liberally over each flan whilst still slightly warm. Transfer to individual serving plates and arrange a few caramelised oranges on each plate. Serve with chantilly cream.

CHANTILLY CREAM

150ml (¹/4 pint) double cream (chilled)
5ml (1 tsp) icing sugar
30ml (2 tbsp) iced water
2 drops of vanilla essence

Put all the ingredients in a chilled bowl and whisk until doubled in volume, about 2 minutes.

Regional Heats

THE NORTH

Sarah Beattie • Jean Hayton • Louise Solden

LOUISE SOLDEN

A teacher of fabric technology, Louise lives just outside Leeds with her jeweller husband and their five year-old son. She is keenly interested in antiques and spends much of her free time at fairs. Louise is particularly fascinated by Art Deco, of which she has a growing collection.

At home she's a demon cake decorator, and is especially fond of children's theme parties where she can let her imagination run wild.

LOUISE SOLDEN'S MENU

STARTER

Salad of Smoked Salmon
with Exotic Fruits and Vegetables in a Sesame Dressing

MAIN COURSE

Stuffed Breast of Chicken in Filo Pastry, served with a Wild
Mushroom Sauce
Tagliatelle with Pecorino and Parmesan
Carrot and Courgette Ribbons in a Coriander and Lime Glaze

DESSERT

Hot Pineapple in a Crème de Cacao Sauce
served with Vanilla Ice Cream

SALAD OF SMOKED SALMON WITH EXOTIC FRUITS AND VEGETABLES IN A SESAME DRESSING

This dish works equally well with prawns and smoked chicken. Any combination of fruit and vegetables can be used according to imagination, availability and pocket. Remember to have a good balance of colour, flavour and texture.

175g (6 oz) smoked salmon
125g (4 oz) mangetouts
125g (4 oz) baby corn
125g (4 oz) cherry tomatoes
1 mango
1 small ripe melon, eg. Ogen
assorted salad leaves, eg. frisée, radicchio, rocket, endive

Dressing:
3-4 spring onions (white part only), chopped
1 small piece fresh root ginger, sliced
4 cloves garlic, sliced
45ml (3 tbsp) sesame oil
15ml (1 tbsp) thin honey
15ml (1 tbsp) dark soy sauce
pinch of Chinese five-spice powder
15ml (1 tbsp) chopped coriander leaves
300ml (1/2 pint) chicken stock
salt and freshly ground black pepper

To make the dressing, lightly sauté the spring onions, ginger and garlic in the sesame oil for 2-3 minutes. Add the remaining ingredients and simmer for 10-15 minutes. Leave to cool, then strain.

Cut the smoked salmon into slivers. Blanch the mangetouts and baby corn in boiling water; drain thoroughly. Halve the cherry tomatoes. Peel the mango and cut into thin slices, discarding the stone. Halve the melon, scoop out the seeds, then scoop the flesh into balls, using a melon baller.

Toss all the salad ingredients in the dressing and serve on large plates.

Stuffed Breast of Chicken in Filo Pastry served with a Wild Mushroom Sauce

Take great care when making the mousse that you keep everything as cold as possible. I prefer to use raw spinach as you get a better colour, but you can blanch it first if you prefer.

A word of warning - you must keep the filo pastry covered with a damp cloth until you are ready to use it or it will dry out.

4 chicken breasts (preferably free-range or corn-fed)
4 sheets of filo pastry
125g (4 oz) butter, melted
1 egg, beaten, to glaze

Mousse:
125g (4 oz) boneless chicken breast or thigh meat
75g (3 oz) spinach leaves
150ml ($^1/4$ pint) double cream
freshly grated nutmeg to taste
salt and freshly ground pepper
15g ($^1/2$ oz) butter
350-450g ($^3/4$-1 lb) wild mushrooms, eg. oyster, shiitake

Sauce:
1.2 litres (2 pints) good homemade chicken stock
Madeira to taste
wild mushrooms(reserved from mousse)
25-50g (1-2 oz) butter

First prepare the mousse. Put the chicken and spinach in a food processor and work until smooth. Pass through a sieve, chill, then add the cream, nutmeg and seasoning. Heat the butter in a pan and sauté the mushrooms for no longer than 1 minute. Set aside three quarters of them for the sauce.

Open out the chicken breasts as flat as possible . Season, then add a spoonful of mousse together with some sautéed mushrooms. Carefully close the chicken breasts and wrap securely in foil. Bring the stock to the boil in a large pan. Add the chicken and poach for 10 minutes. Remove from the stock and leave to cool, then unwrap. Reduce the stock and reserve.

Brush a sheet of filo pastry with melted butter and fold in half. Brush the top again with butter. Place a chicken breast in the centre and wrap the filo around, folding in the ends, to make a parcel. Repeat with the remaining filo and chicken.

Brush the filo parcels with beaten egg and place on a well buttered baking tray. Cook in a preheated oven at 190ºC (375ºF) mark 5 for 25 minutes. Just before you serve, add the Madeira to the chicken stock, and check seasoning. Add the remaining mushrooms and poach briefly, then strain.

Arrange the filo parcels on individual plates with the mushrooms. Whisk the butter into the stock in pieces; serve separately as a sauce.

TAGLIATELLE WITH PECORINO AND PARMESAN

I normally make my own pasta for this dish and have therefore included my homemade pasta recipe below. Alternatively, buy fresh pasta from your local Italian delicatessen.

225g (8 oz) fresh tagliatelle
30ml (2 tbsp) extra virgin olive oil
(approximately)
50g (2 oz) Parmesan cheese, finely grated
50g (2 oz) pecorino cheese, finely grated
15ml (1 tbsp) finely chopped flat-leaved parsley
salt and freshly ground pepper

Cook the pasta in a large pan of boiling water until *al dente*, 1-2 minutes. Drain and refresh the pasta.

Heat the olive oil in a pan, add the pasta, cheeses, parsley and seasoning. Toss lightly and serve.

HOMEMADE PASTA

I have tried all sorts of different recipes for pasta but the one I like best was given to me by David Watson, head chef at Pool Court restaurant in Leeds.

450g (1 lb) strong plain flour
6 whole eggs
4 egg yolks
30ml (2 tbsp) olive oil
salt and freshly ground pepper

Put all the ingredients in a food processor and process for about 2 minutes. Wrap in cling film and leave to rest in the refrigerator for at least 30 minutes.

Roll out the pasta thinly and cut to whatever shape you need - I use a pasta machine for this.

CARROT AND COURGETTE RIBBONS IN A CORIANDER AND LIME GLAZE

225g (8 oz) carrots
225g (8 oz) courgettes
50g (2 oz) butter
2.5ml ($^1/_2$ tsp) ground coriander
2.5ml ($^1/_2$ tsp) sugar
15-30ml (1-2 tbsp) chopped coriander leaves
grated rind of 1 lime
juice of 1 lime
salt and freshly ground pepper

Pare the carrots and courgettes into long thin ribbons, using a potato peeler. Melt the butter in a pan, add the vegetables and sauté for 1-2 minutes. Add the remaining ingredients and cook for 1 minute. Serve immediately.

HOT PINEAPPLE IN A CREME DE CACAO SAUCE

1 small pineapple
25g (1 oz) butter
65ml (2¹/2 oz) dark brown sugar
juice of 1 orange
300ml (¹/2 pint) pineapple juice
60ml (2 fl oz) crème de cacao

Peel and core the pineapple. Cut 4 slices from the middle and set aside; finely chop the rest of the pineapple flesh.

Melt the butter in a large frying pan, add the chopped pineapple and brown sugar, and cook until the mixture caramelises. Slowly add the orange juice and pineapple juice and continue cooking until slightly reduced. Add the crème de cacao and reduce again.

Add the pineapple slices and cook for 2-3 minutes. Transfer the pineapple slices to warmed serving plates, spoon the sauce around them and top each with a scoop of vanilla ice cream.

VANILLA ICE CREAM

3 egg yolks
100g (3¹/2 oz) vanilla sugar
300ml (¹/2 pint) milk
150ml (¹/4 pint) double cream
1 vanilla pod, seeds extracted

Whisk the egg yolks and sugar together until pale and thick. Put the milk and cream into a saucepan, with the vanilla seeds, and bring to the boil. Pour on to the egg mixture, whisking constantly. If you have a microwave oven, transfer the custard to a large bowl and microwave on medium for approximately 3 minutes, until the mixture thickens enough to coat the back of a wooden spoon. Alternatively, pour the custard back into the saucepan and cook gently, stirring constantly, until thickened. Strain the mixture into a clean bowl and allow to cool.

Transfer to an ice-cream maker and churn until thick. Alternatively, pour into a freezerproof container and freeze until firm, whisking every 1-2 hours to improve the texture.

REGIONAL HEATS

THE EAST

AMITA BALDOCK • ROBERT HOWLET • TRICIA HUMBER

—— WINNER ——

AMITA BALDOCK

Formerly a British Airways stewardess, Amita met her husband on a long haul flight and was soon grounded. She now looks after her beautiful two-year-old daughter, Lauren, who models professionally for advertising.

A superb cake decorator, Amita recently met Michel Roux at The Waterside Inn and he was so impressed by her work that he asked her to decorate a cake for his birthday - big enough for fifty portions! Somehow she still finds time for a little gentle windsurfing.

AMITA BALDOCK'S MENU

STARTER

Mussels in Mildly Spiced Coconut Sauce
"CAN I HAVE ANOTHER ONE" SOPHIE GRIGSON

MAIN COURSE

Fillet of Lamb 'En Papillote' with
Rhubarb and Honey Sauce
Spinach and Sorrel Mousse
Baked Red Onions
Sautéed Potatoes in Port

DESSERT

Chilled Jasmine Tea and Cointreau Ice Cream
served in Brandy Snap Baskets
"THAT'S FABULOUS" DAVID GOWER

MUSSELS IN MILDLY SPICED COCONUT SAUCE

I normally use fresh coconut milk, although you can use the canned variety for convenience. To make fresh coconut milk: fill a measuring jug to 450ml ($^3/_4$ pint) with grated fresh coconut, then put into a food processor or blender. Add 300ml ($^1/_2$ pint) very hot water and blend for a few seconds. Line a sieve with muslin and place over a bowl. Empty the contents into the sieve. Gather the corners of the muslin and squeeze out the liquid.

1.75kg (4 lb) mussels
65g (2$^1/_2$ oz) unsalted butter
175g (6 oz) shallots, finely chopped
2 cloves garlic, crushed
2.5cm (1 inch) piece fresh root ginger, grated
1.25ml ($^1/_4$ tsp) turmeric
5ml (1 tsp) ground cumin
250ml (8 fl oz) coconut milk (fresh or canned)
250ml (8 fl oz) chicken stock
salt and freshly ground pepper
15ml (1 tbsp) chopped coriander leaves

Scrub the mussels thoroughly in cold water, discarding any that are damaged or open.

Heat 15ml (1 tbsp) butter in a pan, and fry the shallots until they become translucent. Add the garlic, ginger, turmeric and cumin and fry over moderate heat, stirring continuously, for 5 minutes to thoroughly cook the spices. Add the coconut milk, stock and seasoning. Bring to the boil, then simmer until the sauce has reduced by a third.

Strain the sauce into a large pan. Add the mussels, cover and cook over moderate heat for 4 minutes or until the shells open; discard any unopened mussels. Remove the mussels from the sauce with a slotted spoon and keep warm.

Strain the sauce and reduce over a high heat until it becomes slightly syrupy. Remove from the heat, then whisk in the remaining butter in pieces, a little at a time.

Remove the empty upper shell from each mussel and put the mussels into warmed soup bowls. Pour the desired amount of sauce over the mussels and sprinkle with coriander to serve.

Fillet of Lamb 'En Papillote' with Rhubarb and Honey Sauce

2 fillets of lamb, each about 225g (8 oz)
10ml (2 tsp) Dijon mustard
10ml (2 tsp) olive oil

Pastry:
225g (8 oz) plain flour
pinch of salt
60ml (4 tbsp) finely chopped rosemary
a little water to bind

Rhubarb and Honey Sauce:
450g (1 lb) rhubarb, chopped
30ml (2 tbsp) honey
450ml (³/4 pint) chicken stock
30ml (2 tbsp) port
30ml (2 tbsp) honey
1 stick cinnamon
2 blades of mace
lemon juice to taste
salt and freshly ground pepper
50g (2 oz) unsalted butter, in pieces

To make the pastry, mix the flour, salt and rosemary together in a bowl. Add a little water to bind the pastry, using your hands.

Mix the mustard and oil together and thinly spread all over the lamb fillets.

Divide the pastry into two equal pieces. Roll out one piece on a lightly floured surface until it is just over double the width and length of each lamb fillet. Place a lamb fillet on one side of the pastry. Dampen the edges of the pastry with water and fold the pastry over to enclose the lamb. Press the edges of the pastry together to seal well. Place on an oiled baking tray. Repeat the process with the remaining lamb fillet and pastry. Cook in a preheated oven at 200°C (400°F) mark 6 for 15 minutes.

Meanwhile prepare the rhubarb and honey sauce. Put all the ingredients, except the lemon juice, seasoning and butter, into a pan. Bring to the boil, then simmer until the sauce has reduced and the rhubarb has disintegrated. Pass through a sieve. Add lemon juice and seasoning to taste. Whisk in the butter, a little at a time, over low heat, to give the sauce a gloss. Keep warm.

Remove the lamb from the oven and leave to rest for 5 minutes. Discard the pastry and cut the lamb fillets into slices. Arrange on warmed plates and pour the rhubarb and honey sauce around the lamb to serve.

SPINACH AND SORREL MOUSSE

300ml (¹/2 pint) homemade chicken stock
450g (1 lb) spinach, stalks removed
125g (4 oz) sorrel, stalks removed
60ml (4 tbsp) double cream
1 egg, separated
salt and freshly ground pepper
melted butter for brushing

Bring the stock to the boil in a large pan. Add the spinach leaves and simmer for 4 minutes. Add the sorrel leaves and simmer for a further 2 minutes. Strain, discarding the liquid.

Put the spinach mixture, cream and egg yolk in a food processor or blender and work to a purée. Pass through a sieve. Whisk the egg white until soft peaks form, then fold into the purée. Season to taste.

Lightly butter 4 ramekins or subric moulds and fill them with the mixture. Cover with foil. Place in a bain marie, or roasting tin containing enough boiling water to come halfway up the sides of the moulds. Cook in a preheated oven at 190°C (375°F) mark 5 for 20-25 minutes. To test, insert a wooden skewer into the centre of the mousse; if cooked, it should come out clean.

Run a sharp knife around the inside of each mould and turn out on to individual plates. Brush the mousses with melted butter for a shine.

BAKED RED ONIONS

4 medium red onions
melted butter for brushing
salt and freshly ground pepper

Place the onions in a bain marie, or in an ovenproof dish in a roasting tin containing enough water to come halfway up the sides of the dish. Bake in a preheated oven at 190°C (375°F) mark 5 for 30-40 minutes. Remove the onion skins. Brush the onions with melted butter and sprinkle with salt and pepper to serve.

SAUTÉED POTATOES IN PORT

I find it easier and quicker to cook the potatoes in two batches, using two small frying pans at the same time. This dish must not be made too far in advance or it will loose its crispness.

2 large potatoes
salt
125g (4 oz) clarified butter
port for sprinkling

Peel and thinly slice the potatoes. Pat the potato slices dry, then sprinkle with salt.

Melt 25g (1 oz) butter in each small frying pan over high heat. Arrange a quarter of the potato slices in each pan, overlapping in a round, to form a 'pancake'. When the potatoes are golden underneath, lower the heat and cook gently for 4-5 minutes. Turn the 'pancake' over and fry for a further 5 minutes.

Sprinkle with port to taste and remove from the pan. Keep warm while cooking the other two pancakes. Serve immediately.

CHILLED JASMINE TEA AND COINTREAU ICE CREAM

150ml (¹/₄ pint) jasmine tea
150ml (¹/₄ pint) milk
150ml (¹/₄ pint) single cream
2 long strips of pared orange zest
6 egg yolks
125g (4 oz) caster sugar
150ml (¹/₄ pint) double cream
75ml (5 tbsp) Cointreau

To Decorate:
2 oranges, peeled and segmented(all pith removed)

Put the tea, milk, single cream and orange zest into a pan. Gently heat to just below boiling point; do not boil or the taste of the tea will be impaired. Remove the orange zest and set aside.

Meanwhile, whisk the egg yolks and sugar together until pale, thick and creamy. Slowly pour on the milk mixture, stirring all the time. Pour the mixture into a clean pan. Cook very gently over a low heat, stirring continuously,until the custard is thick enough to coat the back of a wooden spoon, about 15-20 minutes.

Strain the custard into a bowl over ice, to cool it quickly. Put back the orange peel. Stir occasionally during cooling. Whisk the double cream and Cointreau together until soft peaks form, then fold into the cooled custard. Take out the orange zest.

Pour the mixture into an ice cream maker and churn for 30-40 minutes; the ice cream is ready to serve. Alternatively, pour the mixture into a freezerproof container and freeze until semi-frozen. Whisk the mixture and return to the freezer until firm. Transfer the ice cream to the refrigerator 30 minutes before serving, to soften.

To serve, scoop the ice cream into brandy snap baskets and decorate with orange segments.

BRANDY SNAP BASKETS

25g (1 oz) butter, softened
50g (2 oz) caster sugar
50g (2 oz) golden syrup
25g (1 oz) plain flour, sifted

Cream the butter and sugar together. Stir in the syrup, then stir in the flour. Place a tablespoonful of the mixture on a greased baking tray. Dip a fork into cold water, then pat the mixture lightly until it is evenly flattened.

Place in a preheated oven at 200°C (400°F) mark 6 for 4-5 minutes, until the mixture has spread and is golden in colour. Quickly slide a palette knife under the brandy snap and carefully mould over an inverted greased small dish to shape the basket. Repeat the process to make 4 baskets in total. Remove from the moulds when cool.

REGIONAL HEATS

THE EAST

AMITA BALDOCK • ROBERT HOWLET • TRICIA HUMBER

ROBERT HOWLETT

R obert lives with his wife, also a doctor, and their young daughter in the pretty village of Great Bardfield in Essex. He is a GP in the nearby practice. To keep himself in good shape, Robert has built a gym in his house and can often be found running at high speed through the village.

Robert's interest in cookery began at university, where he used to compete with the other students with whom he shared a house. He now does most of the cooking at home.

ROBERT HOWLETT'S MENU

STARTER

Parma Ham and Pears with Grapefruit and Ginger Mayonnaise

MAIN COURSE

Boeuf en Croûte with Smoked Oysters
Hot Raw Beetroot
Steamed Carrot Julienne
Steamed Baby Corn
"THAT'S A GOOD WHOLESOME MEAL" LOYD
"A VERY BRITISH COMBINATION" SOPHIE GRIGSON

DESSERT

Exotic Fruits in Grand Marnier, served in Brandy Snap Baskets

PARMA HAM AND PEARS WITH GRAPEFRUIT AND GINGER MAYONNAISE

1 ripe Comice pear
squeeze of lemon juice
16 fine slices of Parma ham (prosciutto)
selection of salad leaves (radicchio, frisée, etc)

Grapefruit and Ginger Mayonnaise:
2 egg yolks
juice of 1/2 grapefruit
1cm (1/2 inch) piece fresh root ginger, grated
150-175ml (5-6 fl oz) sunflower oil
salt and freshly ground pepper

First prepare the mayonnaise. Put the egg yolks in a food processor or blender with 30ml (2 tbsp) grapefruit juice and the ginger. Process for 30 seconds. With the machine running, slowly add the oil through the feeder tube until the mixture is the consistency of mayonnaise. Taste and add seasoning and extra grapefruit juice to taste. Chill.

Peel, halve and core the pear. Cut into neat slices and immerse in a bowl of cold water, with the lemon juice added, to preserve the colour. Drain just before serving.

Arrange the Parma ham, salad leaves and pear slices on individual plates and serve with the chilled mayonnaise.

BOEUF EN CROUTE WITH SMOKED OYSTERS

Use well hung fillet steaks, and a good quality stock for the sauce. To ensure the fillet steaks are perfectly cooked, it is essential to chill the parcels before baking, and to serve them as soon as they are cooked. When cut open, the fillet steaks should be pink inside.

4 fillet steaks, each about 150g (5 oz)
25g (1 oz) butter
4 shallots, finely chopped
450g (1 lb) packet puff pastry
105g (3 1/2 oz) can smoked oysters, drained and chopped
15-30ml (1-2 tbsp) finely chopped parsley
1 egg yolk, beaten, to glaze

Sauce:
1.2 litres (2 pints) good quality beef stock (made from 2 marrow bones)
30-45ml (2-3 tbsp) Madeira
50g (2 oz) butter, chilled
salt and freshly ground pepper
lemon juice to taste

Trim the fillet steaks. Heat the butter in a frying pan, add the steaks and seal very quickly on both sides, then remove. Add the shallots to the pan and sauté until lightly browned; remove.

HOT RAW BEETROOT

Divide the pastry into 4 equal pieces. Roll out each piece on a lightly floured surface to a rectangle, about 25 x 12cm (10 x 5 inches). Place a steak on one side of each pastry rectangle and top with the chopped oysters, shallots and parsley. Brush the edges of the pastry with beaten egg yolk. Fold the pastry over the steak and press the edges together to seal. Use a 15cm (6 inch) fluted cutter to cut these edges into a scallop shape.

Brush all over with beaten egg yolk and decorate with leaves cut from the pastry trimmings. Place the parcels on a lightly buttered baking sheet and chill for 1 hour.

Meanwhile, heat the stock in a saucepan and simmer until reduced to about 150ml (1/4 pint) and thickened. Flavour with the Madeira.

Bake the parcels in a preheated oven at 220°C (425°F) mark 7 for 20 minutes until the pastry is crisp and golden.

Shortly before the steaks are cooked, add the butter, in pieces, to the stock, a little at a time, whisking constantly. Season and add lemon juice to taste. Serve the steak parcels as soon as they are cooked, with the sauce, and vegetable accompaniments.

Either use canned concentrated orange juice, available frozen; or reduce 150ml (5 fl oz) freshly squeezed orange juice to 15ml (1 tbsp) by boiling.

450g (1 lb) raw young beetroot
15ml (1 tbsp) walnut oil
15ml (1 tbsp) concentrated orange juice
salt and freshly ground pepper

Finely grate the beetroot. Heat the walnut oil in a wok or frying pan, add the beetroot and concentrated orange juice and stir-fry for 6 minutes. Season with salt and pepper to taste. Serve immediately.

EXOTIC FRUITS IN GRAND MARNIER

A medley of exotic fruits, topped with fromage frais and cream, crushed Amaretti and grated dark chocolate.

1 ripe mango
225g (8 oz) cape gooseberries
225g (8 oz) seedless black grapes
Grand Marnier to taste

To Serve:
4 brandy snap baskets (see below)
170ml (6 fl oz) double cream
170ml (6 fl oz) fromage frais
handful of Amaretti biscuits, crushed
finely grated rind of 1 orange
25-50g (1-2 oz) quality dark chocolate, finely grated

Peel the mango and dice, discarding the stone. Remove the papery husks from the cape gooseberries. Halve the grapes. Place the fruit in a bowl and add a splash of Grand Marnier to taste. Leave to marinate for about 1 hour.

Whisk the double cream until thick, then fold in the fromage frais.

Just before serving, pile the fruit into the brandy snap baskets. Spoon the cream mixture over the fruit and top with crushed Amaretti biscuits, grated orange rind and chocolate.

BRANDY SNAP BASKETS

50g (2 oz) unsalted butter
50g (2 oz) golden syrup
50g (2 oz) caster sugar
50g (2 oz) plain flour

Heat the butter, syrup and sugar in a pan over low heat until dissolved. Remove from the heat and stir in the flour. Place a tablespoon of the mixture on a baking sheet lined with lightly buttered baking parchment. Using dampened fingers, spread into a very thin, slightly irregular 15cm (6 inch) circle.

Bake in a preheated oven at 190°C(375°F) mark 5 for about 6 minutes until browned —not burnt! Immediately peel the brandy snap off the paper and carefully mould over an inverted greased ramekin to shape the basket. Repeat to make 4 baskets. Remove from the ramekins when cool.

Regional Heats
THE EAST
Amita Baldock • Robert Howlet • Tricia Humber

TRICIA HUMBER

Tricia is one of four daughters all of whom are great 'foodies', and her collection of cookery books is massive. She works as a freelance marketing consultant in the food and drink business, and lives with husband Robin in Leighton Buzzard. They are both fascinated by food markets which they study on their frequent travels abroad.

Tricia is also enamoured by trains, both the model variety which are set up in her cellar, and the narrow gauge steam type which runs around Leighton Buzzard.

TRICIA HUMBER'S MENU

STARTER
Carrot and Coriander Soup
Cheese Straws
"BEAUTIFUL COLOUR — NICE IDEA" LOYD

MAIN COURSE
Noisettes of Spring Lamb in a Madeira and Cream Sauce
Spring Greens with Onions
Buttered Swede Balls
Steamed Leeks
Saffron Rice

DESSERT
Blackberry and Cassis Fool
Almond Pastry Twists
"THAT WOULD GO DOWN IN A HURRY, I PROMISE YOU" DAVID GOWER

CARROT AND CORIANDER SOUP

If fresh coriander isn't available, use parsley instead.

30ml (2 tbsp) olive oil
1 small onion, finely chopped
1 clove garlic, crushed
450g (1 lb) carrots, chopped
5ml (1 tsp) crushed coriander seeds
5ml (1 tsp) ground coriander
900ml (1¹/₂ pints) vegetable stock
salt and freshly ground pepper
15ml (1 tbsp) chopped coriander
coriander leaves to garnish

Heat the olive oil in a pan and sauté the onion and garlic until softened. Add the carrots and cook gently for 10 minutes. Add the crushed coriander seeds and ground coriander and cook for a further 2 minutes. Pour in the vegetable stock, bring to the boil, then cover and simmer for 15 minutes.

Purée the soup in a food processor or blender, then season with salt and pepper to taste. Reheat if necessary. Stir in the chopped coriander and pour into warmed individual bowls. Garnish with coriander leaves and serve with cheese straws.

CHEESE STRAWS

125g (4 oz) ready-made puff pastry
1 egg yolk, mixed with a little water
50g (2 oz) Cheddar Cheese, finely grated
25g (1 oz) freshly grated Parmesan cheese

Roll out the pastry to a rectangle, 3mm (¹/₈ inch) thick, on a lightly floured surface. Trim the edges. Brush the pastry with the egg yolk, then sprinkle evenly with the grated cheeses. Lightly roll to press the cheeses on to the pastry. Cut into strips, 10cm (4 inches) long and 1cm (¹/₂ inch) wide.

Place the pastry strips on a greased baking sheet and bake in a preheated oven at 200°C (400°F) mark 6 for 7 minutes or until golden brown. Transfer to a wire rack and leave to cool.

NOISETTES OF SPRING LAMB IN A MADEIRA AND CREAM SAUCE

12 small best end of neck lamb chops, boned
12 small rosemary twigs (with sprigs of leaves at the top)
pinch each of dried marjoram, sage, thyme and oregano
120ml (8 tbsp) olive oil
15g (1/2 oz) butter
5ml (1 tsp) coarsely chopped rosemary leaves
120ml (8 tbsp) Madeira
90ml (6 tbsp) double cream
salt and freshly ground pepper

Trim the fat from the lamb, then fold the tail of each chop around the eye of the meat to form a noisette. Using a skewer, spike each noisette, then insert a rosemary twig to hold each noisette together. Ensure that the twig protrudes sufficiently so that the noisette does not unwrap during cooking.

Mix the dried herbs with half of the olive oil in a shallow dish. Add the noisettes and rub well with the marinade. Cover and leave to marinate at room temperature for at least 1 hour, turning occasionally.

Pour off the olive oil marinade into a heavy pan and add the remaining olive oil. Heat the oil, then add the noisettes and fry, turning frequently, for about 5-6 minutes or until cooked but still slightly pink in the centre. Remove, drain and keep warm.

Melt the butter in the pan and add the chopped rosemary. Pour in the Madeira, then add the cream, stirring well to avoid catching. Season and reduce slightly. Strain to remove any pieces of rosemary, then return to the pan and continue to reduce to a fairly thick sauce.

To serve arrange the lamb, with the rosemary twigs still in, on warmed serving plates. Pour the sauce over and around the noisettes. Serve immediately.

SPRING GREENS WITH ONIONS

Select the youngest, smallest and most tender Spring greens you can find for this accompaniment. Alternatively you can use young spinach or cabbage leaves.

450g (1 lb) Spring greens
1 small onion, finely chopped
15ml (1 tbsp) olive oil
freshly grated nutmeg
salt and freshly ground black pepper

Finely slice the spring greens and steam over boiling water until tender. Meanwhile sauté the onion in the olive oil until tender. Remove with a slotted spoon and keep warm.

Once the greens are cooked, drain and toss with the onion. Season with nutmeg, salt and pepper to taste.

Lightly grease 4 ramekins or individual moulds and spoon in the mixture. Press down firmly to exclude any air pockets. Cover with foil and leave to stand in a warm oven until ready to serve. Invert on to warmed serving plates and turn out carefully. Serve immediately.

BUTTERED SWEDE BALLS

450g (1 lb) swede
25g (1 oz) butter
30ml (2 tbsp) single cream or milk
10ml (2 tsp) sugar
salt and freshly ground pepper

Chop the swede and steam over boiling water until tender. Drain and mash, adding the butter, cream or milk, sugar and salt and pepper to taste.

To serve, scoop into balls, using an ice cream scoop.

STEAMED LEEKS

450g (1 lb) small leeks
25g (1 oz) butter
salt and freshly ground pepper

Clean the leeks thoroughly and slice thinly, crosswise. Steam over boiling water until just tender; avoid turning them too much or they will break up. Once cooked, drain and toss gently in the butter. Season with salt and pepper to taste. Serve immediately.

SAFFRON RICE

pinch of saffron strands, coarsely crushed
225g (8 oz) Basmati Rice
pinch of salt
25g (1 oz) butter
300ml (¹/2 pint) water
15ml (1 tbsp) finely chopped chives

Infuse the saffron strands in 30ml (2 tbsp) boiling water for at least 10 minutes. Strain the liquid and set aside; reserve the strands for garnish.

Rinse the rice in cold water to remove excess starch. Place in a saucepan with the salt, saffron liquid, butter and water. Bring to the boil, cover tightly and simmer over a very gentle heat for 10 minutes, until the rice is cooked and the water is absorbed.

Lightly mix in the chopped chives. Transfer to a warmed serving bowl and garnish with some of the reserved saffron strands to serve.

Note: To keep warm, cover with buttered foil to keep the rice moist and place in a low oven.

BLACKBERRY AND CASSIS FOOL

450g (1 lb) blackberries
175g (6 oz) sugar
60ml (4 tbsp) water
60ml (4 tbsp) crème de cassis
300ml (¹/₂ pint) double cream, chilled
icing sugar for dusting

Set aside 4 good blackberries for decoration.

Put the rest of the blackberries in a saucepan with the sugar and water. Cover and cook gently for 20 minutes or until the fruit is pulpy. Leave to cool for 10 minutes, then sieve to remove the blackberry pips.

Pour the cassis into 4 individual glasses or a large serving bowl and chill.

Whip the cream until stiff peaks form, then fold in the blackberry purée until evenly combined. Carefully spoon the mixture into the serving glasses or bowl, keeping the cassis at the bottom. Chill for at least 1 hour.

Decorate with the reserved fruit and dust with icing sugar. Serve with almond pastry twists.

ALMOND PASTRY TWISTS

125g (4 oz) ready-made puff pastry
50g (2 oz) sugar
50g (2 oz) blanched almonds, finely chopped
1 egg yolk, mixed with a little water

Roll out the pastry to a rectangle, 3mm (¹/₈ inch) thick, on a lightly floured surface. Trim the edges. Mix the sugar with the almonds. Brush the pastry with egg yolk, then sprinkle evenly with half of the sugar and almond mixture. Lightly roll to press the coating on to the pastry, then carefully turn the pastry over. Brush with egg yolk and sprinkle with the remaining sugar and almond coating. Roll lightly.

Cut into strips, 10cm (4 inches) long and 5mm (¹/₄ inch) wide. Hold both ends of each strip and twist in opposite directions. Place the twists on a greased baking sheet, pressing both ends of each twist on to the baking sheet to prevent curling.

Bake in a preheated oven at 200°C (400°F) mark 6 for 5 minutes. Transfer to a wire rack and leave to cool.

THE SOUTH WEST

ROGER ASHBY • ADRIAN BREGAZZI • JULIET DONNER

—————— WINNER ——————

ROGER ASHBY

A company director from Sidford, Roger has lived in Devon for sixteen years. He started his own Satellite TV Company in 1984, and the next year won the Best Technical Business Award. He is married with five children ranging from the age of two to twenty three.

Some twelve years ago Roger started a campaign for a swimming pool to be built in Sidmouth. This is now under construction, and due to open in January '92.

Roger's cooking centres on game and fish, most of which comes from a nearby Vivier.

ROGER ASHBY'S MENU

STARTER
Langoustines in Noilly Prat and Cream Sauce

MAIN COURSE
Filleted Saddle of Exmoor Venison with Madeira Sauce
Turnip and Redcurrant 'Tartlets'
Baby Roast Potatoes
Demi-purée of Carrots and Swede
Curly Kale

DESSERT
Pear and Crème Anglaise Flan with Devonshire Cream
"THAT'S EXCEPTIONALLY GOOD THAT TART" LOYD

LANGOUSTINES IN NOILLY PRAT AND CREAM SAUCE

1.75kg (4 lb) live langoustines (Dublin Bay prawns)

Sauce:
1.4kg (3 lb) fish bones and trimmings (preferably sole, halibut or plaice)
25-75g (1-3 oz) butter
1 leek, chopped
1 onion, chopped
1 carrot, chopped
1/2 stick celery, chopped
125g (4 oz) mushrooms, chopped
salt and freshly ground pepper
150ml (1/4 pint) dry white wine
900ml (1 1/2 pints) water
2 sprigs parsley
250ml (8 fl oz) double cream
60ml (2 fl oz) Noilly Prat
squeeze of lemon juice

Wash the langoustines in a large colander under running water. Drop into a large pan of salted water on a rolling boil. Allow the water to return to a simmer and cook the langoustines for no longer than 4 minutes. Drain and cool. Set aside 4 whole langoustines for garnish. Remove the heads and claws from the rest of the langoustines and reserve; leaving tail meat in shell.

To prepare the sauce, clean the fish bones and trimmings thoroughly. Heat 25g (1 oz) butter in a pan, add the vegetables with a few grinds of pepper and sweat for 3-4 minutes; do not allow to brown. Add the fish trimmings, with the heads and claws of the langoustines, and the wine. Boil for 4 minutes to expel the alcohol. Add the water and parsley. Cover and simmer gently for 40 minutes.

Strain the sauce into a clean pan and reduce to 300ml (1/2 pint).

Meanwhile, shell the langoustine tails. Cut the tail meat in half lengthwise and remove the black intestinal vein if present. Arrange the halves in a fir-tree shape on large warmed plates.

To finish the sauce, add the cream and Noilly Prat. Correct the seasoning and cut with a dash of lemon juice. If the sauce is too thin, whisk in the remaining butter (chilled) a little at a time, until the desired consistency is reached.

Garnish each plate with a whole langoustine, with claws upright. Spoon the sauce over the langoustine tails to serve.

FILLETED SADDLE OF EXMOOR VENISON WITH MADEIRA SAUCE

This is worth doing with wild venison and well made stock. If you are thinking of a stock cube stop now!

1.75kg (4 lb) saddle joint of young venison
a little dried rosemary
8 juniper berries
pork fat strips for covering, or clarified butter for brushing
300ml (¹/2 pint) dark chicken stock
90ml (3 fl oz) Madeira

Turnip and Redcurrant 'Tartlets':
4 baby turnips
450g (1 lb) fresh or frozen redcurrants
125g (4 oz) sugar

Using a very sharp knife, cut 2 fillets from the top side of the saddle, each 20cm (8 inches) long, 5cm (2 inches) in diameter. Crush the juniper berries and position along the top of the fillets, with a sprinkling of dried rosemary. Cover with a thin layer of pork fat, or brush with clarified butter. Place in a roasting tin.

To prepare the turnip and redcurrant 'tartlets', simmer the whole baby turnips in salted water for about 15 minutes until tender. Carefully cut off the tops and reserve. Using a melon baller, scoop out the inside flesh to make 'tartlets'. Heat the redcurrants with the sugar in a pan, to a thick consistency; do not allow the berries to break down.

Meanwhile, cook the venison fillets in a preheated oven at 220ºC (425ºF) mark 7 for 8-10 minutes. Remove from the roasting pan, cover and leave to rest in a warm place.

Combine the stock with the Madeira and add to the roasting pan, stirring to deglaze. Separate off any fat, then strain the sauce.

Spoon the redcurrants into the warm turnips and replace the tops to surprise your guests.

Carve the venison obliquely to give oval slices; it should be pink in the centre. Arrange the venison on warmed serving plates. Add any juices from the meat to the sauce, then spoon around the venison. Garnish with the turnip and redcurrant 'tartlets'.

Serve with baby potatoes sautéed in clarified butter, a demi-purée of carrot and swede, and curly kale.

PEAR AND CRÈME ANGLAISE FLAN

Always leave Devonshire clotted cream at room temperature for 2 hours before serving to allow the flavour to develop.

Sweet Flan Pastry:
250g (9 oz) plain flour
pinch of salt
125g (4 oz) butter, softened
125g (4 oz) icing sugar
2 eggs

Filling:
4 medium pears
sugar syrup for poaching (see note)

Crème Anglaise:
300ml (¹/₂ pint) milk
1-2 vanilla pods, split
3 egg yolks
150g (5 oz) caster sugar

To Serve:
granulated sugar for sprinkling
Devonshire clotted cream

To make the sweet flan pastry, sift the flour and salt on to a marble slab or work surface. Make a well in the centre and add the butter in pieces, icing sugar and eggs. Gradually mix the flour into the other ingredients to form a soft dough. Knead lightly, then wrap in cling film and chill in the refrigerator for 30 minutes.

Roll out the pastry on a lightly floured surface and use to line a 20cm (8 inch) loose-bottomed flan tin. Prick the base and chill for 20 minutes. Line with greaseproof paper and baking beans and bake blind in a preheated oven at 200°C (400°F) mark 6 for 15 minutes. Remove paper and beans and bake for a further 5 minutes.

Meanwhile, peel, halve and core the pears, leaving the stalks intact. Poach in the sugar syrup until just tender. Drain.

In the meantime, make the crème Anglaise. Put the milk and split vanilla pods in a saucepan and heat gently to just below simmering point. Beat the eggs with the sugar until light and creamy. Pour on the hot milk, beating constantly. Strain into a double boiler or a heatproof bowl over a pan of simmering water and cook, stirring, until the custard is thick enough to coat the back of a spoon.

Drain the pear halves and slice into fans, leaving them attached at the stalk end. Arrange in the flan case, with the stalks 'sitting up'. Pour on the crème anglaise and bake at 180°C (350°F) mark 4 for 20-30 minutes until set.

Allow to cool, then sprinkle lightly with granulated sugar. Serve with clotted cream.

Note: To make the sugar syrup, dissolve 200g (7 oz) sugar in 1.2 litres (2 pints) water over low heat, then bring to the boil and allow to simmer for 5 minutes.

REGIONAL HEATS
THE SOUTH WEST
ROGER ASHBY • ADRIAN BREGAZZI • JULIET DONNER

ADRIAN BREGAZZI

A drian lives in the Cornish town of Falmouth where he is marketing manager of the Arts College, and deeply involved with computer generated 3-D graphics.

Away from the screen, Adrian likes to cycle along the Cornish coastal roads and often takes his two daughters bird watching at the nearby National Trust sanctuary.

ADRIAN BREGAZZI'S MENU

STARTER
Red Mullet in Red Jackets

MAIN COURSE

Roast Boned Quail stuffed with Chicken, Shiitake and Smoked Bacon
Gratin of Leeks, Potatoes and Pears
Carrots with Orange and Cardamom Sauce
Steamed Courgette Tagliatelle
"IF THERE WAS A PIN-UP MAGAZINE FOR VEGETABLES..." LOYD

DESSERT
Tart Orange and Lemon Ice Cream with a Bitter Chocolate Sauce
"THAT'S SPECTACULAR" GLENYS KINNOCK
"IT'S BRILLIANT, BRILLIANT" RICK STEIN

RED MULLET IN RED JACKETS

4 small or 2 large red mullet
2 large red-ripe tomatoes
a little walnut oil
freshly grated nutmeg
about 20 saffron strands
160ml (5^1/$_2$ fl oz) fish stock
75ml (3 fl oz) chicken stock
30ml (2 tbsp) Noilly Prat
30ml (2 tbsp) double cream
50g (2 oz) unsalted butter
6-8 basil leaves, torn

To Garnish:
10ml (2 tsp) chopped chives
10ml (2 tsp) chervil leaves

Carefully clean and fillet the red mullet removing the scales; reserve the liver. Pick out any residual bones from the fillets with tweezers. Cut each small fillet into 2 pieces; cut large fillets into 4. Chop or pound livers.

Peel the tomatoes. Cut 1 tomato into 8 wedges, discarding the seeds and steam for 3 minutes; or microwave on high for 1 minute. Allow to cool. Halve and seed the other tomato; finely chop the flesh and reserve for the sauce.

Lightly oil a large heatproof plate with walnut oil. Arrange half of the red mullet fillets, side by side and skin side down on the plate. Dot the pounded liver along the centre line and sprinkle with a little nutmeg. Cover with the tomato segments. Place the remaining red mullet fillets on the plate, skin side up. Cover and leave in the refrigerator until needed.

Soak the saffron strands in 45ml (3 tbsp) fish stock for about 1 hour. Bring the rest of the fish stock to the boil. Add the chopped tomato flesh and simmer for 10 minutes until the stock is coloured. Pass through a fine sieve into another saucepan. Add the chicken stock and saffron with its liquid. Simmer, covered, for 20 minutes. Add the Noilly Prat and cream, reduce a little, then gradually add the butter in pieces, with the torn basil leaves, stirring well.

Steam the red mullet fillets for 3 minutes or microwave, covered, on high for 1 minute. Carefully arrange the fish pieces - two with tomatoes, two skin side up - on warmed serving plates. Pour a little of the sauce on to each serving and sprinkle with chives and chervil. Serve immediately.

Roast Boned Quail stuffed with Chicken, Shiitake and Smoked Bacon

4 free-range French quails, part-boned
(leaving only leg and wing bones)
4 rashers smoked bacon, derinded
5ml (1 tsp) freshly ground allspice
salt and freshly ground black pepper

Stuffing:
4 fresh shiitake mushrooms, finely
chopped
15g (^{1}/2 oz) unsalted butter
100g (3^1/2 oz) boneless chicken breasts
60ml (4 tbsp) double cream
1 large egg
10ml (2 tsp) finely chopped parsley
20ml (4 tsp) finely chopped red pepper

To Baste:
50-75g (2-3 oz) unsalted butter, melted

To Garnish:
30ml (2 tbsp) shredded grapefruit zest
juice of 1 grapefruit
15ml (1 tbsp) sugar

Lay out the boned quails, flesh-side uppermost, on a work surface. Lay a strip of bacon on the skin of each quail, between the breast fillets and overlapping the rump end by about 2.5cm (1 inch). Dust with allspice and pepper.

To prepare the stuffing, sauté the shiitake mushrooms in the butter until softened. Coarsely chop the chicken flesh and place in a food processor with the cream and egg. Process until smooth. Transfer to a bowl and stir in the parsley, red pepper and shiitake mushrooms. Season with salt and pepper.

Divide the stuffing between the quails and reassemble by pulling the skin together. Secure with cocktail sticks and truss with fine string. Brush liberally with melted butter. Cook in a preheated hot oven at 200ºC (400ºF) mark 6 for 25-30 minutes, basting frequently.

Meanwhile blanch the grapefruit zest in 3 changes of boiling water. Drain and place in a saucepan with the grapefruit juice and sugar. Cook over moderate heat until lightly caramelised.

Remove the quail from the oven and leave to rest for 10 minutes before removing the string and cocktail sticks. Serve garnished with the caramelised grapefruit zest.

GRATIN OF LEEKS, POTATOES AND PEARS

90ml (6 tbsp) finely chopped leeks
30ml (2 tbsp) fresh white breadcrumbs
2 cloves garlic
5ml (1 tsp) freshly grated nutmeg
2 potatoes, about 200g (7 oz), coarsely grated
2 pears, about 200g (7 oz), finely grated
60ml (4 tbsp) double cream

To Finish:
60ml (4 tbsp) melted butter

Combine all of the ingredients for the gratin in a bowl and mix evenly. Divide between two well buttered 10cm (4 inch) flan tins and dribble the melted butter over the surface.

Cook in a preheated oven at 220°C (425°F) mark 7 for 20 minutes. Halve and serve immediately.

CARROTS WITH ORANGE AND CARDAMOM SAUCE

90ml (6 tbsp) diced carrots
90ml (6 tbsp) fresh carrot juice
juice of 1 orange
90ml (6 tbsp) chicken stock
65g (2¹/2 oz) unsalted butter
freshly ground cardamom seeds for sprinkling

Place the carrots in a saucepan with the carrot juice, orange juice and chicken stock. Cook over medium heat until tender and well glazed. Add the butter and toss well. Serve topped with a sprinkling of ground cardamom.

STEAMED COURGETTE TAGLIATELLE

4 courgettes, each 12cm (6 inches) long
30ml (2 tbsp) freshly grated Parmesan cheese

Peel the courgettes and cut lengthwise into long fine slices. Steam over boiling water for 5 minutes. Drain and serve sprinkled with Parmesan.

Tart Orange and Lemon Ice Cream with a Bitter Chocolate Sauce

Ice Cream:
4 small mineolas, or other small oranges
2 eggs, separated
75g (3 oz) caster sugar
finely grated rind and juice of 2 lemons
finely grated rind of 2 oranges
300ml ($^1/_2$ pint) double cream
juice of 1 lime

Bitter Chocolate Sauce:
200g (7 oz) bitter chocolate
30ml (2 tbsp) brandy or Cointreau
60ml (4 tbsp) double cream
1 small coffee-cup strong black coffee
(espresso)

To Decorate:
60ml (4 tbsp) single cream
shredded lemon zest, blanched
16 fine raspberries

To prepare the mineolas or oranges, slice off their tops and trim their bases to a flat surface. Scoop out as much flesh and pith as possible, then place the orange shells in the freezer.

Whisk the egg yolks with the caster sugar until pale and thick. Add the grated lemon and orange rinds. In another bowl, whip the cream until thick, then slowly add the lime juice and nearly all of the lemon juice.

Whisk the egg white until soft peaks form. Fold the whipped cream into the egg yolk mixture, then carefully fold in the egg white. Transfer to a freezerproof container and place in the freezer for 30 minutes.

Transfer to an ice-cream maker and churn for 15 minutes. Alternatively, whisk by hand. Spoon the ice cream into the mineola or orange shells and freeze until firm.

To make the bitter chocolate sauce, combine the chocolate, brandy or Cointreau, cream and half of the coffee in a heavy-based saucepan. Stir over a moderate heat until smooth. Cool, then adjust the consistency as necessary by adding more (cooled) coffee. Leave in the refrigerator until required.

To assemble, pour out a little pool of chocolate sauce on to each serving plate and carefully position the ice cream filled oranges in the centre. Spoon 4 drops of cream on the plate (at 12, 3, 6, and 9 o'clock), streak with the tip of a knife, then mount each with a raspberry. Sprinkle with lemon zest to serve.

REGIONAL HEATS
THE SOUTH WEST

ROGER ASHBY • ADRIAN BREGAZZI • JULIET DONNER

JULIET DONNER

Juliet lives on a magnificent 500 acre estate at Whitchurch in Hampshire which is managed by her husband. The house itself is huge and rambling. When we asked Juliet what she did with her time she said she spent most of it looking for things she had lost the day before! Hopefully these did not include her two sons, her retrievers or the family cat.

When she does manage some time to herself, Juliet generally reaches for her paints and a canvas.

JULIET DONNER'S MENU

STARTER
Surprise Fish Parcels with Dill Sauce

MAIN COURSE
Medallions of Lamb with Lentils, and Bramble and Wine Sauce
Bonfire of Vegetables
"THE SAUCE IS VERY NICE — DELICATE" RICK STEIN

DESSERT
Sunset Strawberries with Redcurrant Sauce
"LIKE AN INTELLECTUAL'S VERSION OF STRAWBERRY SHORTCAKE"
LOYD

SURPRISE FISH PARCELS WITH DILL SAUCE

1 medium salmon tail
1 monkfish tail
small handful of finely chopped dill
salt and freshly ground pepper
65g (2^1/$_2$ oz) butter

Dill Sauce:
250ml (8 fl oz) crème fraîche
150ml (^{1}/$_4$ pint) soured cream
3 spring onions, chopped
small handful of finely chopped dill

To Garnish:
dill sprigs

Fillet the salmon and remove the skin. Remove the outer membrane from the monkfish, then cut out the bone. Cut the monkfish into discs, about 5mm (^{1}/$_4$ inch) thick, and roll in finely chopped dill to coat. Lay one salmon fillet on your work surface. Cover with the dill-coated monkfish and season with salt and pepper. Top with the other salmon fillet.

Slice into 4 portions and place a knob of butter on each one. Place each portion on a piece of baking parchment and steam over boiling water until tender, about 10 minutes. Lift out each portion as it is cooked; thicker portions may take a little longer.

While the fish is cooking, make the sauce. Gently mix the crème fraîche with the soured cream, spring onions and dill. Season with a little pepper.

To serve, carefully transfer the fish parcels to individual serving plates. Tear the paper in the middle and remove, so that the cooking juices are left on the plate. Garnish with dill and serve immediately, accompanied by the dill sauce.

MEDALLIONS OF LAMB WITH LENTILS, AND BRAMBLE AND WINE SAUCE

If possible, use a mixture of lentils, such as green and brown ones.

700-900g (1^1/$_2$-2 lb) lamb fillets (boned loins), depending on size
olive oil for marinating
handful of rosemary sprigs
125g (4 oz) lentils
3-4 cloves garlic
30ml (2 tbsp) olive oil
4-5 chestnut mushrooms, sliced
125g (4 oz) bramble jelly
60ml (2 fl oz) light red wine

Cut the lamb fillets into 2.5cm (1 inch) thick medallions. Rub with olive oil, add rosemary sprigs and leave to marinate for 1-2 hours. Meanwhile, cook the lentils in boiling water with 1 garlic clove added for 35 minutes or until tender. Drain and keep warm.

Heat the oil in a heavy-based frying pan. Add 2-3 crushed garlic cloves and plenty of rosemary sprigs to flavour, then add the mushrooms and cook gently until softened. Remove and keep warm. Increase the heat and add the lamb to the pan. Seal over high heat, turning, then lower the heat and cook for about 7 minutes.

Meanwhile, put the bramble jelly and red wine in a pan with a large sprig of rosemary and heat gently until melted; do not allow to boil.

To serve, arrange a 'bonfire of vegetables' on one side of each serving plate. Add a portion of lentils, then arrange the meat and mushrooms on top. Spoon a little of the bramble and wine sauce around the lamb and lentils. Serve immediately, with the remaining sauce handed separately.

ANGELA JAQUES' DESSERT (SEMI-FINAL)

Pear Clafoutis with Poire Williem Sorbet

ROGER ASHBY'S MAIN COURSE (SEMI-FINAL)

Fillet of Hare in a Port Sauce with Pears and Blackcurrants
Pot-Roasted Baby Potatoes
Kohlrabi, Broccoli and Carrots

BONFIRE OF VEGETABLES

Use vegetables in season for this accompaniment, varying your choice according to availability.

2 large potatoes
salt and freshly ground pepper
2 large carrots
2 parsnips
2 courgettes
knob of butter

Cook the potatoes in boiling salted until tender. Meanwhile cut the carrots, parsnips and courgettes into julienne strips, 5mm (¼ inch) thick and 5cm (2 inches) long. Steam the vegetable julienne in individual baking parchment compartments, over boiling salted water until tender. Remove each compartment of vegetables when cooked and drain.

Drain the potatoes and mash with butter until smooth.

To serve, place a mound of creamed potato on each serving plate and pile the vegetable julienne around it to resemble an unlit bonfire. Serve immediately.

SUNSET STRAWBERRIES WITH REDCURRANT SAUCE

225g (8 oz) strawberries

Hazelnut Biscuits:
50g (2 oz) shelled hazelnuts
125g (4 oz) plain flour
50g (2 oz) butter, melted

Topping:
grated dark and white chocolate (chilled)

Redcurrant Sauce:
225g (8 oz) redcurrants
handful of strawberries
45ml (3 tbsp) sugar
5 ml (1 tsp) potato flour

To Serve:
a little single cream

To make the hazelnut biscuits, crush the hazelnuts with a rolling pin. Mix together the flour, butter and hazelnuts to a smooth dough. Wrap in cling film and chill in the refrigerator for 30 minutes.

Roll out the dough quite thinly on a lightly floured surface. Using an inverted glass or pastry cutter, cut out half-moon shapes. Transfer to a baking sheet and bake in a pre-heated oven at 200ºC (400ºF) mark 6 for 7 minutes. Cool on a wire rack.

To make the redcurrant sauce, put the redcurrants in a saucepan with a little water. Cook until softened. Press through a sieve into a clean pan. Purée the strawberries in a blender or food processor, then sieve to remove pips.

Mix the potato flour with a little water, then add to the redcurrant sauce and cook gently until the sauce has thickened slightly. Stir in the strawberry purée and sugar. Allow to cool.

To assemble, sprinkle grated chocolate over the hazelnut biscuits. Slice the strawberries and arrange on top of the biscuits. Place on individual dessert plates and surround with the redcurrant sauce. Using a teaspoon, drizzle a crescent of cream on to each pool of sauce and feather using the tip of a knife to resemble sun rays. Serve immediately.

REGIONAL HEATS
THE NORTH WEST
SUE LONGDEN • MALCOLM HAWE • LYNDA HINTON

WINNER

SUE LONGDEN

All three of the North West regional finalists come from a small area around Blackpool. Sue is a supply chemistry teacher, and lives with her husband and three young children in the pretty village of Poulton-le-Fylde. She is an enthusiast photographer, particularly of the children, and a collector of blue and white china, especially 'objets' large enough to contain members of her considerable orchid collection.

SUE LONGDEN'S MENU

STARTER
*Mangetouts stuffed with Poached Salmon,
served with Speckled Tomato Vinaigrette*

MAIN COURSE
*Chicken Moroccan-style
Mixed Rice Timbales
Baked Cherry Tomatoes*
"IT'S A BIT LIKE SENDING YOUR TONGUE HITCH-HIKING" LOYD
"OOHH, THAT'S VERY YUMMY" ANGELA RIPPON

DESSERT
Hazelnut Biscuits with Toffee Apples and Cassis

MANGETOUTS STUFFED WITH POACHED SALMON, SERVED WITH SPECKLED TOMATO VINAIGRETTE

This tastes as beautiful as it looks. Try to choose mangetouts of an even size and prepare a few extra, in case you damage the pods when you fill them. The keta-speckled tomato vinaigrette looks particularly attractive. Keta is the orangey-pink roe of a Pacific salmon; you could use red lumpfish roe instead.

225g (8 oz) salmon fillet
a little fish stock for poaching
20 mangetouts (plus a few spares)
5ml (1 tsp) low-fat soft cheese
(approximately)
5ml (1 tsp) mayonnaise (approximately)
5ml (1 tsp) chopped dill
salt and freshly ground pepper
squeeze of lemon juice
50g (2 oz) smoked salmon fillets
4 chives

Tomato Vinaigrette:
225g (8 oz) large, ripe tomatoes, or cherry tomatoes
pinch of salt
pinch of caster sugar
5ml (1 tsp) balsamic vinegar
freshly ground white pepper
30-45ml (2-3 tbsp) olive oil
5-10ml (1-2 tsp) keta (salmon roe)

First prepare the tomato vinaigrette. Whizz the tomatoes in a food processor, then sieve to remove skins and seeds. Add the salt, sugar, vinegar and pepper to taste. Whisk in the olive oil. Stir in the keta.

Lightly poach the salmon fillet in a little stock until just opaque; do not overcook. Remove with a slotted spoon.

Blanch the mangetouts in boiling water for 1 minute, then drain and refresh in cold water; drain. Using a sharp knife, carefully split each mangetout pod down one side, then slide your finger inside and open up to make a pocket. This isn't as difficult as it sounds!

Place the salmon in a bowl and mash with a fork, adding the soft cheese and mayonnaise to soften the texture. Stir in the dill, seasoning and lemon juice to taste. If you prefer a smoother texture you can work the mixture briefly in a food processor.

Using a small spoon, push some of the salmon mixture into the cavity of each mangetout pod. Cut the smoked salmon into 4 strips and roll each piece around a spoonful of the salmon mixture, then tie with a chive.

To serve, pour a little vinaigrette on to each plate and spread thinly to show off the speckles of caviar. Arrange 5 stuffed mangetouts and a smoked salmon roll on each pool of sauce. Serve immediately.

CHICKEN MOROCCAN-STYLE

Do use free-range chicken for this and don't be tempted to use chicken breasts, because they haven't the succulency to carry this robustly flavoured sauce. The deliciously perfumed blend of flavourings is inspired by a Moroccan tajine. It includes preserved lemon - a Moroccan speciality - which is easy to prepare.

6-8 chicken thighs (depending on size)

Stuffing:
30ml (2 tbsp) chopped coriander
30ml (2 tbsp) chopped parsley
1 preserved lemon (see note)
10ml (2 tsp) ground cumin
freshly ground black pepper
8 green olives, stoned
3 cloves garlic
30ml (2 tbsp) olive oil

Marinade:
large pinch of saffron strands
300ml (¹/₂ pint) boiling water

Sauce:
125ml (4 fl oz) white wine
15ml (1 tbsp) chopped coriander
15ml (1 tbsp) chopped parsley
15g (¹/₂ oz) stoned green olives, cut into slivers
few slivers of preserved lemon rind (see note)
150ml (¹/₄ pint) double cream
salt and freshly ground pepper
squeeze of lemon juice (optional)

Using sharp kitchen scissors, bone the chicken thighs. Put the bones in a roasting tin and brown in a preheated oven at 180°C (350°F) mark 4 for 30-45 minutes.

Meanwhile, put all the stuffing ingredients in a blender or food processor and work until the mixture is well blended. Spread a little of this mixture over the inside of each chicken thigh, roll up and tie loosely if necessary with fine strings. Place in a shallow dish.

Steep the saffron strands in the boiling water for about 10 minutes, then strain the liquid over the chicken and leave to marinate for several hours, turning occasionally.

Remove the chicken from the marinade, wipe dry and place in the roasting tin with the bones; reserve 150ml (¹/₄ pint) marinade. Roast the chicken in the oven for 25-30 minutes until cooked through and crispy on the outside; increase the heat towards the end of the cooking time if necessary. Discard the bones. Transfer the chicken to a warmed plate; keep warm.

Deglaze the pan with the wine. Add the reserved marinade and allow to bubble over a medium heat until syrupy. Strain if necessary, then add the herbs, olives, preserved lemon rind and a little cream. Simmer until rich and creamy. Check the seasoning and add a little lemon juice if preferred.

To serve, slice the chicken. Pour a pool of sauce on to each serving plate and arrange the chicken slices on top. Serve immediately.

Note: To prepare lemon preserve, wash and dry 450g (1 lb) unwaxed lemons, then cut lengthwise into quarters, leaving them attached at the base. Sprinkle 30-45 ml (2-3 tbsp) salt over the insides. Reshape and pack into a small sterilized jar. Fill to the brim with cooled boiled water, seal and store in a cool place for about 3 weeks.

MIXED RICE TIMBALES

Use a small metal mould, coffee cup or similar container for these timbales. Use the same container to measure the rice.

2/3 measure wild rice
2 measures white long-grain rice
600ml (1 pint) light chicken stock or
water (approximately)
knob of butter
2 spring onions, finely chopped

Cook each type of rice separately in about 300ml ($1/2$ pint) chicken stock; the white rice will take about 10 minutes, the wild rice 50-55 minutes. Rinse with cold water to arrest cooking; drain thoroughly. Just before serving, combine both types of rice with the butter and spring onions. Heat through gently, stirring, then press a quarter of the mixture into the warmed mould. Turn out on to a warmed serving plate. Repeat to make 3 more timbales. Serve immediately.

Note: I've recently discovered boxes of mixed wild and plain white rice, which by some alchemy can be cooked together!

BAKED CHERRY TOMATOES

24 even-sized cherry tomatoes
(approximately)
large handful of basil leaves
2.5ml ($1/2$ tsp) coriander seeds
2.5ml ($1/2$ tsp) fennel seeds
salt and freshly ground pepper
extra virgin olive oil for drizzling

Pierce each tomato in a few places with a fine skewer to prevent the skins bursting during cooking. Lay the tomatoes on a bed of basil leaves, tucking a few more basil leaves in between them. Coarsely crush the coriander and fennel seeds and mix with salt and pepper. Sprinkle evenly over the tomatoes and drizzle with olive oil. Bake in a preheated oven at 180ºC (350ºF) mark 4 for 10 minutes.

HAZELNUT BISCUITS WITH TOFFEE APPLES AND CASSIS

This dessert looks more elegant if you scoop the apple flesh into balls with a melon baller. You will need the extra apple if you choose to prepare them in this way.

Pastry:
175g (6 oz) butter (at room temperature)
50g (2 oz) caster sugar
225g (8 oz) plain flour
175g (6 oz) roasted hazelnuts, ground

Toffee Apples:
3-4 Granny Smith apples
50g (2 oz) butter
50g (2 oz) soft brown sugar

To Finish:
150ml (1/4 pint) double cream
icing sugar for dusting
60-90ml (4-6 tbsp) crème de cassis
violet flowers to decorate

For the pastry, put all the ingredients into a food processor and process until the dough is beginning to hold together. Immediately switch off the machine, form the dough into a ball and chill for 30 minutes.

Roll out the pastry on a lightly floured surface to a little less than 5mm (1/4 inch) thickness. Cut out 12 circles, using a 7.5 cm (3 inch) cutter; this allows for breakages. Transfer to a baking sheet lined with non-stick paper and bake at 180°C (350°F) mark 4 for 7 minutes. Carefully transfer to a wire rack to cool.

Peel, halve and core the apples, then cut into slices or scoop the flesh into small balls, using a melon baller, if you want to be flash! Set aside a few pieces for decoration.

Melt the butter in a heavy-based pan, add the sugar, then the apples. Cook gently until the apples are caramelised and toffee-like. Allow to cool.

Whip the cream until thick. To assemble, sandwich the biscuits together in pairs with the cream and toffee apples. Dust the top biscuits with icing sugar. Spread a pool of crème de cassis on each serving plate and place a hazelnut biscuit in the centre. Decorate with the reserved apple and violets to serve.

Regional Heats
The North West
Sue Longden • Malcolm Hawe • Lynda Hinton

Malcolm Hawe

Malcolm is managing director of a house building company with prize-winning estates throughout Britain. He lives in Preston with his Wife, Glad, who is the interior designer of many of the company's show homes. They have five children, of whom four are adopted and come from distant lands.

Despite an extremely high pressure life, Malcolm never misses his Friday night football matches, and recently he aggregated 13 under par on the Fairhaven Golf Course. He takes his cooking equally seriously, and last year enjoyed a holiday at a cookery school in France.

Malcolm Hawe's Menu
Starter
Seafood with Fruit Hors D'Oeuvre

Main Course
Lamb with Port and Redcurrant Sauce
Pommes Parisienne
Sautéed Mangetouts and Carrots
"THAT'S EXACTLY HOW IT SHOULD BE — A GREAT TASTE OF OLIVES"
EUGENE McCOY

Dessert
Poached Peaches in Caramel Cages
"SORT OF LIKE A GROWN-UP PECHE MELBA" LOYD

SEAFOOD WITH FRUIT HORS D'OEUVRE

4 quails' eggs
paprika for sprinkling
1 small cooked lobster, in portions

Smoked Salmon and Avocado Mousse:
1 avocado
75ml (5 tbsp) mayonnaise
75ml (5 tbsp) double cream
7.5ml (1¹/2 tsp) lemon juice
7g (¹/4 oz) powdered gelatine
salt and freshly ground pepper
75g (3 oz) smoked salmon slices

Fruit Coulis:
1 mango
1 kiwi fruit

Cherry Tomato Flowers:
4 cherry tomatoes
chives
herb leaves

Orange Butter Sauce:
juice of 1¹/2 oranges
50g (2oz) unsalted butter

To Garnish:
4 orange segments

To prepare the smoked salmon and avocado mousse, peel, halve and stone the avocado and chop roughly. Purée with a little water in a blender or food processor. Transfer to a bowl and stir in the mayonnaise, cream and lemon juice. Dissolve the gelatine in 30ml (2 tbsp) hot water, then add to the avocado mixture. Season with salt and pepper to taste.

Line the base and sides of 4 small moulds with two thirds of the smoked salmon. Fill with the avocado mousse and cover with the remaining smoked salmon. Chill until firm.

To prepare the mango coulis, peel, halve and stone the mango, then purée in a blender or food processor. Purée the kiwi fruit, then sieve to remove the pips, for the kiwi coulis.

To make each cherry tomato flower, place stalk end down and carefully cut through the skin only, marking it into 8 petals. Using the tip of the knife, carefully peel back the petals. Decorate with herbs.

To prepare the orange butter sauce, simmer the orange juice until reduced to 15ml (1 tbsp). Gradually whisk in the butter, a little piece at at time. Keep warm.

Place the quails' eggs in a saucepan, add cold water to cover and bring to the boil. Boil for 2 minutes, then plunge into cold water to cool. Peel and cut off the tops to reveal the yolks. Sprinkle with paprika.

To serve, set each quails' egg in a portion of mango coulis on a large serving plate. Carefully unmould the salmon and avocado mousses and set in a portion of kiwi coulis on the plate. Arrange a portion of lobster with a segment of orange alongside and spoon on a little orange butter sauce. Finally, position the cherry tomato flowers.

LAMB WITH PORT AND REDCURRANT SAUCE

4 portions best end of lamb (about 3 chops per portion)
50g (2 oz) clarified butter
salt
30ml (2 tbsp) olive oil

Port and Redcurrant Sauce:
150ml (1/4 pint) port
125g (4 oz) redcurrant jelly
juice of 1 orange
juice of 1/2 lemon
5ml (1 tsp) mustard powder
5ml (1 tsp) arrowroot

Cut out the 'eye' of the chops, removing fat and sinew. Rub with clarified butter and season with salt. Heat the oil in a frying pan and fry the lamb, turning, for a few minutes on each side, until browned on the outside, but still pink in the middle.

To prepare the sauce, put the port and redcurrant jelly in a saucepan and heat gently until dissolved. Add the orange and lemon juices. Stir in the mustard. Blend the arrowroot with a little water and add to the sauce. Heat, stirring, until the sauce thickens.

Cover about a quarter of each serving plate with the sauce. Slice the lamb thinly and arrange the slices overlapping in a fan shape on the sauce. Form a small circle of pommes parisienne with a cherry tomato in the centre on each plate. Neatly and carefully arrange the mangetouts and carrots, then serve.

POMMES PARISIENNE

450g (1 lb) potatoes
salt and freshly ground pepper
50-75g (2-3 oz) clarified butter

Peel the potatoes and scoop the flesh into small potato balls using a melon baller. Season with salt and pepper. Heat the clarified butter in a roasting tin, add the potato balls and roast in a preheated oven at 180°C (350°F) mark 4 for about 40 minutes. Serve immediately.

SAUTÉED MANGETOUTS AND CARROTS

225g (8 oz) baby carrots (preferably with stalks)
salt
225g (8 oz) mangetouts
50g (2 oz) clarified butter

Cook the carrots in boiling salted water to cover for 4 minutes. Drain, then sauté in half of the clarified butter for 30 seconds. Sauté the mangetouts in the remaining clarified butter for 30 seconds. Serve immediately, to ensure that vegetables retain their crispness.

POACHED PEACHES IN CARAMEL CAGES

4 large firm ripe peaches

Sugar Syrup:
175g (6 oz) caster sugar
300ml (¹/₂ pint) water

Sauce:
425g (15 oz) can peach slices, drained
squeeze of lemon juice

Caramel Cages:
150ml (¹/₄ pint) water
350g (12 oz) lump sugar
10ml (2 tsp) liquid glucose

To Decorate:
30ml (2 tbsp) double cream
4 mint leaves

To make the sugar syrup, put the sugar and water in a heavy-based pan and heat gently until the sugar is dissolved, then bring to the boil and simmer for 5 minutes.

Add the peaches to the sugar syrup and poach at simmering point for about 20 minutes or until soft. Leave in the syrup to cool. Reserve 60ml (2 fl oz) syrup for the sauce.

To make the sauce, purée the canned peach slices in a blender or food processor with the reserved sugar syrup. Pass through a sieve to yield a smooth sauce, then add lemon juice to taste.

To prepare the caramel for the cages, put the water, lump sugar and glucose in a heavy-based pan and heat gently until the sugar has dissolved. Bring to the boil and simmer until the syrup reaches the hard crack stage: 155°C (305°F) on a sugar thermometer. To test, drop a little of the syrup into a cup of cold water - it should separate into hard, brittle threads. Remove from the heat and dip the pan into cold water to arrest the cooking process.

Oil the back of a ladle with sunflower oil. Take a teaspoonful of caramel and trickle a thin thread, backwards and forwards, side to side and around the base of the ladle; it will set very quickly. When set, very gently remove the cage from the ladle and place in an airtight container until ready to use. Repeat to make three more cages.

When ready to assemble, lift the peaches out of the syrup. Remove their skins, halve and stone, then reshape as whole peaches.

To serve, spread a pool of sauce on each serving plate. Add dots of cream around the perimeter and feather with the tip of a knife. Place a peach in the centre of the sauce. Top with a mint leaf and carefully place a caramel cage over the top of each peach.

REGIONAL HEATS
THE NORTH WEST

SUE LONGDEN ● MALCOLM HAWE ● LYNDA HINTON

LYNDA HINTON

Lynda's home is in Lytham St Annes. Like many a mother, a major part of her life is spent looking after her offspring, but in her daughter Katie's case it is because she is one of Britain's most successful young riders. When not training or driving to shows, Lynda writes for the British Show Pony Society magazine.

Formerly the manager of a beauty salon, Lynda now owns and runs an electrical contracting company, mainly involved in lighting for pubs, clubs and hotels. When does she find time to cook?

LYNDA HINTON'S MENU

STARTER
Mushrooms in Brandy Sauce, served with Herb Bread

MAIN COURSE
*Baby Halibut served with a Tangy Almond Sauce in
a Pastry Shell
Parsnips with Ricotta and Soured Cream
Cauliflower Fritters
Pommes Noisettes*
"THERE'S A NICE SHARP BITE TO THAT"   ANGELA RIPPON

DESSERT
French Apple Flans with Raspberry Coulis

MUSHROOMS IN BRANDY SAUCE

This dish is superb as a starter or as an accompaniment to vegetarian burgers or well-grilled liver or kidneys. I use chestnut mushrooms because they have a delicious nutty flavour. Have crusty bread on hand to mop up the juices.

350g (12 oz) chestnut mushrooms
salt and freshly ground pepper
25g (1 oz) butter
a sprinkling of flour
125ml (4 fl oz) brandy
125ml (4 fl oz) double cream
15ml (1 tbsp) chopped parsley

Roughly chop the mushrooms and season with pepper. Melt the butter in a frying pan, add the mushrooms and sauté for 2-3 minutes, stirring constantly. Sprinkle with a little flour and cook, stirring, for 30 seconds.

Add the brandy over a high heat and cook for 1-2 minutes to reduce. Lower the heat and stir in the cream and parsley. Season with salt and pepper.

Transfer to warmed individual serving dishes and serve with herb bread

HERB BREAD

Any combination of herbs can be used to suit the accompanying dish.

1 French stick
50-75g (2-3 oz) butter, softened
15-30ml (2-3 tbsp) finely chopped mixed herbs (e.g. parsley and tarragon)

Cut the French stick diagonally into slices without cutting right through to the base. Mix the softened butter with the herbs until evenly blended. Spread the French bread slices with the herb butter and reassemble the loaf into its original shape. Wrap in foil and heat through in a preheated oven at 200°C (400°F) mark 6 for 10 minutes.

BABY HALIBUT SERVED WITH A TANGY ALMOND SAUCE IN A PASTRY SHELL

350g (12 oz) packet puff pastry
8 fillets of baby halibut, each 125g-175g (4-6 oz), skinned
salt and freshly ground pepper
45ml (3 tbsp) lemon juice
65g (2$\frac{1}{2}$ oz) ground almonds
300ml ($\frac{1}{2}$ pint) chicken stock
1 clove garlic, crushed
7.5ml ($\frac{1}{2}$ tbsp) turmeric
15ml (1 tbsp) chopped parsley

To Glaze:
1 egg yolk; beaten with 15ml (1 tbsp) milk

To Garnish:
lemon wedges
dill or parsley sprigs
salad leaves
cherry tomatoes

Roll out the pastry to a 5mm (1/4 inch) thickness on a lightly floured surface. Cut out 4 fish shapes, using a fish template measuring 12-15cm (6-7 inches) long and 10cm (4 inches) wide. Lightly mark a line just inside the edge of each pastry shape; this will form a lid after baking. Leave to rest in the refrigerator for at least 20 minutes.

Season the halibut fillets with salt and pepper and 15ml (1 tbsp) lemon juice. Roll up and place in a greased ovenproof dish. Cover with foil.

Brush the pastry shapes with the egg glaze and bake in a preheated oven at 220°C (425°F) mark 7 for about 12 minutes. When cooked, cut round the line you previously marked, slip the knife underneath and carefully lift off the lids. Transfer pastry cases and lids to a wire rack and keep warm.

Lower the oven temperature to 180°C (350°F) mark 4 and bake the fish for 15-18 minutes until tender.

Meanwhile, put the remaining lemon juice, ground almonds, stock, garlic, turmeric and parsley in a saucepan and bring to the boil, stirring. Simmer for about 10 minutes until thickened. Season with salt and pepper to taste.

Drain the cooked fish and put 2 fillets in each pastry case. Spoon the sauce over the fish. Replace the lids. Garnish with lemon wedges, dill or parsley sprigs, salad leaves and sliced cherry tomatoes to serve.

Note: Make sure the oven temperature has dropped to the correct setting before cooking the fish.

PARSNIPS WITH RICOTTA AND SOURED CREAM

825g (1³/4 lb) parsnips
3 spring onions, chopped
75g (3 oz) ricotta cheese
150ml (1/4 pint) soured cream
25g (1 oz) gruyère cheese, grated
15ml (1 tbsp) fresh white breadcrumbs
salt and freshly ground pepper
freshly grated nutmeg

Cut the parsnips into 5mm (1/4 inch) slices and place in a saucepan. Add salted water to cover, bring to the boil and simmer for 2-3 minutes; drain thoroughly.

Mix the spring onions with the ricotta until evenly blended. Layer the parsnips, ricotta mixture and soured cream in a buttered ovenproof dish, seasoning each layer liberally with salt and pepper and finishing with a layer of soured cream. Scatter the gruyère, breadcrumbs and nutmeg over the top. Cover and cook in a preheated oven at 180°C (350°F) mark 4 for 45-50 minutes, removing the lid for the last 10 minutes to brown the tops.

CAULIFLOWER FRITTERS

These fritters are enveloped in a crispy, light, dry fritter batter, which coats the food only lightly.

825g (1³/4 lb) cauliflower
salt
30ml (2 tbsp) olive oil
15ml (1 tbsp) lemon juice
oil for deep frying

Fritter Batter:
125g (4 oz) plain flour
1¹/2 eggs
22ml (1¹/2 tbsp) olive oil
2.5ml (¹/2 tsp) salt
125ml (4 fl oz) light beer

To Garnish:
parsley sprigs

To prepare the fritter batter, put the flour, eggs, oil and salt in a bowl and beat thoroughly with a wooden spoon until well mixed. Stir in the beer and leave the batter to stand for at least 2 hours before use.

Cut off the stem of the cauliflower and remove the outer leaves. Bring a saucepan of salted water to the boil, put in the cauliflower and simmer until almost tender. Drain, then immediately refresh in cold water; drain and separate into florets. Pat dry with a cloth. Put the florets into a bowl, add the oil and lemon juice and carefully mix together, then leave for 15 minutes before cooking.

Heat the oil in a deep fryer until it is very hot. Dip the cauliflower florets into the batter, one at a time, then deep fry in batches in the hot oil until they are golden brown and float to the surface. Drain on kitchen paper. Sprinkle with salt and serve at once garnished with parsley.

POMMES NOISETTES

1kg (2 lb) potatoes
walnut oil for shallow frying
salt

Peel the potatoes and scoop the flesh into balls, using a melon baller. Immerse in a bowl of cold water until ready to use. Drain and pat dry. Heat the oil in a frying pan, then add the potatoes and fry until golden brown all over and cooked through. Drain on kitchen paper. Sprinkle with salt and serve.

FRENCH APPLE FLANS WITH RASPBERRY COULIS

Pastry:
225g (8 oz) plain flour
pinch of salt
175g (6 oz) butter or margarine
2 egg yolks
50g (2 oz) caster sugar

Pastry Cream:
2 egg yolks
50g (2 oz) caster sugar
22g ($^3/_4$ oz) plain flour
300ml ($^1/_2$ pint) milk
few drops of vanilla essence

Filling:
2 dessert apples, eg Cox's Orange Pippin, Jonagold
apricot jam, warmed and sieved, to glaze
dash of Calvados
40g ($1^1/_2$ oz) caster sugar
ground cinnamon for dusting

Raspberry Coulis:
350g (12 oz) raspberries
100ml ($3^1/_2$ fl oz) cooled sugar syrup (see note)
juice of $^1/_2$ lemon

To Decorate:
few raspberries

To make the pastry, sift the flour and salt into the food processor bowl. Cut the butter or margarine into small pieces, add to the bowl and process for 10-15 seconds. Add the egg yolks and sugar and process for 20 seconds. Wrap in cling film and leave to rest in the refrigerator for 30 minutes.

To make the pastry cream, whisk the egg yolks and sugar together until pale. Fold in the flour. Heat the milk in a saucepan to just below simmering point, then pour onto the egg mixture, whisking constantly. Strain into a clean pan and cook, stirring, until thickened. Add vanilla essence to taste. Cover with a sheet of dampened greaseproof paper or a sprinkling of sugar to prevent a skin forming and leave to cool.

Roll out the pastry thinly and use to line 4 individual 10cm (4 inch) loose-bottomed flan tins. Spread a layer of cooked pastry cream in each flan case. Peel, core and finely slice the apples and arrange on the pastry cream. Sprinkle with the Calvados, then the caster sugar and cinnamon. Bake in a preheated oven at 200°C (400°F) mark 6 for 15 minutes.

Meanwhile, prepare the raspberry coulis. Purée the raspberries in a food processor or blender with the syrup and lemon juice. Sieve to remove pips.

Brush the apple flans with apricot glaze. Spoon a little raspberry coulis on to one side of each serving plate, add a few dots of cream and feather with the tip of a knife. Place a warm flan alongside, but not touching the coulis. Decorate with a few raspberries and serve the remaining coulis separately.

Note: To make a sugar syrup, put 240g ($8^1/_2$ oz) sugar in a heavy-based pan with 450ml ($^3/_4$ pint) water and 40g ($1^1/_2$ oz) powdered glucose. Place over high heat, stirring occasionally with a wooden spoon, until dissolved. Bring to the boil and leave to bubble for several minutes, skimming the surface if necessary. Pass through a conical sieve into a bowl and leave to cool. Once cold the sugar syrup can be kept for up to 2 weeks in a refrigerator and used in any fruit sorbet.

THE FIRST

SEMI-FINAL

AMITA BALDOCK • ANGELA JAQUES • JENNIFER TWYDELL

WINNER

AMITA BALDOCK'S MENU

STARTER
Oysters with Raspberry Sauce
"IT'S ABSOLUTELY STUNNING...AWFULLY GOOD" DEREK NIMMO
"IT'S QUITE DELICIOUS" SALLY CLARKE

MAIN COURSE
Wood Pigeons with Wild and Brown Rice Stuffing, and
Juniper and Port Sauce
Tagliatelle of Vegetables
"VERY, VERY, VERY, VERY UNDERSTATED JUNIPER AND
PORT SAUCE" LOYD

DESSERT
Hot Pear and Banana Filos with Vanilla and Butterscotch
Sauces

OYSTERS WITH RASPBERRY SAUCE

16 oysters
25g (1 oz) shallots, finely chopped
50g (2 oz) unsalted butter
15ml (1 tbsp) raspberry vinegar
15ml (1 tbsp) raspberry purée
30ml (2 tbsp) double cream
30ml (2 tbsp) medium dry white wine
salt and freshly ground white pepper
50g (2 oz) fine French beans
25g (1 oz) mushrooms, finely chopped

To Garnish:
coarse sea salt
raspberries

Open the oysters over a bowl to collect the juice. Lay the oysters on kitchen paper and set aside. Strain the juice.

Gently fry the shallots in a little of the butter until soft, but not coloured. Add the oyster juice, vinegar and raspberry purée. Cook over a high heat until reduced and syrupy. Add the cream and wine. Let the sauce bubble briefly, then remove from the heat and beat in the rest of the butter, a little at a time. Adjust the seasoning.

Cut the French beans into 1cm ($^1/_2$ inch) lengths and boil until tender but still crisp; drain. Refresh under cold water, drain and cut into julienne. Set aside half of the beans for garnish; add the rest to the sauce.

Boil the empty deeper halves of the oyster shells to clean and warm them. Set the shells on warmed plates lined with sea salt.

Add the chopped mushrooms and oysters to the sauce and place over a medium heat. As soon as the sauce starts to tremble, spoon into the oyster shells.

Garnish with the julienne of French beans and raspberries to serve.

WOOD PIGEONS WITH WILD AND BROWN RICE STUFFING, AND JUNIPER AND PORT SAUCE

4 wood pigeons

Stuffing:
25g (1 oz) wild rice
175g (6 oz) brown rice
25g (1 oz) butter
2 rashers streaky bacon, finely chopped
1 shallot, finely chopped
grated rind of 1 orange
25g (1 oz) walnuts, skinned and finely chopped
salt and freshly ground pepper
15-30ml (1-2 tbsp) chopped coriander leaves

Sauce:
30ml (2 tbsp) oil
50g (2 oz) butter
1 onion, chopped
4 juniper berries, crushed
few thyme sprigs
300ml (1/2 pint) homemade stock
125ml (4 fl oz) port
15ml (1 tbsp) redcurrant jelly
salt and freshly ground pepper

Wash and dry the pigeons.

For the stuffing, wash the wild rice and brown rice separately. Cook the wild rice in boiling salted water in a covered pan for 30 minutes or until tender; drain. Heat the butter in a pan, add the bacon and shallot and sauté until the shallot is softened. Add the brown rice and cook, stirring continuously, until the rice becomes translucent. Add 275 ml (9 fl oz) water and bring to the boil, then simmer covered for 20-25 minutes or until the rice is tender. Add the orange rind, wild rice, walnuts, seasoning and coriander.

To make the sauce, heat the oil and half of the butter in a pan and quickly seal the pigeons, then remove. Add the onion to the pan and fry until softened. Stir in the juniper berries, thyme, stock and port and bring to the boil. Simmer until the sauce has reduced by half. Strain the sauce into a clean pan. Add the redcurrant jelly and stir over moderate heat until the jelly has melted. Beat in the remaining butter, a little at a time, and adjust the seasoning. Keep warm.

Stuff the pigeons with the rice mixture and truss with fine string. Place in a roasting dish. Cook in a preheated oven at 220°C, (425°F) mark 7 for 20-25 minutes or until tender. Remove the string. Place the pigeons on individual warmed plates and spoon over the sauce to serve.

TAGLIATELLE OF VEGETABLES

2 carrots
2 courgettes
1 leek
125ml (4 fl oz) water
125g (4 oz) butter
salt and freshly ground pepper

Peel the carrots and cut them in half lengthwise. Using a potato peeler, cut the carrots into long ribbons. Cut the ribbons into 5mm (1/4 inch) strips. Repeat the process with the courgettes. Halve the leek lengthwise, then cut into 5mm (1/4 inch) strips.

Put the water and butter in a pan and bring to the boil. Add the leek, then add the carrots and cook until the carrots are tender but still crisp. Turn off the heat and add the courgettes. Strain, sprinkle with seasoning to taste and serve immediately.

HOT PEAR AND BANANA FILOS WITH VANILLA AND BUTTERSCOTCH SAUCES

2 pears
2 bananas
squeeze of lemon juice
pinch of ground cinnamon
4 sheet filo pastry
melted butter for brushing

Vanilla Sauce:

4 egg yolks
40g (1^1/2 oz) sugar
150ml (^{1}/4 pint) milk
150ml (^{1}/4 pint) single cream
1 vanilla pod, split

Butterscotch Sauce:

50g (2 oz) butter
75g (3 oz) soft brown sugar
50g (2 oz) golden syrup
125ml (4 fl oz) double cream

To Finish:

icing sugar for dusting

To make the vanilla sauce, whisk the egg yolks and sugar together until pale, thick and creamy. Put the milk, cream and vanilla pod in a pan and bring to the boil. Pour on to the whisked mixture, stirring all the time. Return to a clean pan and cook gently over a low heat, stirring continuously, until the sauce thickens. Remove the vanilla pod, strain the sauce and allow to cool.

To make the butterscotch sauce, put all the ingredients, except the cream, into a pan and bring to the boil. Remove from the heat and whisk in the cream. Return to the heat and bring to the boil. Strain the sauce and set aside.

To prepare the filos, peel, halve and core the pears, then chop and place in a bowl. Slice the bananas, add to the bowl and sprinkle with lemon juice and cinnamon. Toss gently. Take a sheet of filo pastry and lightly butter one half, then fold in half. Place a quarter of the fruit mixture in the middle and brush the edges of the filo with melted butter. Gather up the corners of the pastry and twist together to seal. Place the fruit filo on a greased baking tray. Repeat the process until you have 4 fruit filos.

Bake in a preheated oven at 190ºC (375ºF) mark 5 for 10-15 minutes or until the filo pastry is crisp and golden brown.

Place the fruit filos on individual plates and dust with icing sugar. Serve with cold vanilla sauce and hot butterscotch sauce.

THE FIRST
SEMI-FINAL

AMITA BALDOCK • ANGELA JAQUES • JENNIFER TWYDELL

ANGELA JAQUES' MENU

STARTER
Pan-fried Tomatoes

MAIN COURSE
Lamb with Rosemary and Olive Sauce
Hot Green Bean and Hazelnut Salad
Mashed Potatoes with Celeriac
"THE ROSEMARY IS JUST PERFECT...A VERY GOOD SAUCE" LOYD

DESSERT
Pear Clafoutis with Poire William Sorbet

Pan-fried Tomatoes

These are sensational and almost too easy!

4 beefsteak tomatoes
60ml (4 tbsp) best quality virgin olive oil
4 pinches of sugar
20ml (4 tsp) chopped chervil
2 cloves garlic, chopped

Halve the tomatoes crosswise and scoop out the seeds. Pat dry with kitchen paper. Heat the olive oil in a heavy skillet or cast iron frying pan and place the tomatoes, face down, in the pan. Cook on the lowest possible heat for 40 minutes. Carefully turn over and sprinkle each tomato with sugar, chervil and garlic, then trickle a little oil over the top. Continue cooking gently for 30-40 minutes... *courage mon brave*, I assure you they will not burn but transform into something sensational! Serve with crisp French bread and 'dunk' greedily.

Lamb with Rosemary and Olive Sauce

2 best ends of lamb, filleted
5ml (1 tsp) chopped shallot
2.5ml ($^1/_2$ tsp) chopped rosemary
125g (4 oz) pitted black olives, rinsed
15ml (1 tbsp) white wine
30ml (2 tbsp) oil
2 egg yolks
22g ($^3/_4$ oz) butter, melted
60ml (4 tbsp) cream

To Garnish:
rosemary sprigs

Trim the lamb if necessary. Purée the shallot, rosemary, olives and wine in a food processor or blender, then place in a small pan over low heat and melt slowly for 10 minutes. Press through a sieve into a heatproof bowl above a pan of boiling water.

Heat the oil in a skillet or heavy-based frying pan and quickly sear the lamb to seal on all sides. Transfer to a greased baking sheet and cook in a preheated oven at 200ºC (400ºF) mark 6 for 8 minutes.

Meanwhile return to your sauce and whisk in the egg yolks. Continue whisking until you have a thicker and creamier mixture. During this time, the lamb will need to be removed from the oven. Leave it to rest in a warm place for 10 minutes. Very gradually whisk the melted butter into the sauce, to yield a thick glossy sauce. Thin down with cream to a light pouring consistency.

To serve, slice the lamb and arrange on individual plates. Trickle the sauce over the edge of the slices. Garnish with rosemary and serve immediately.

HOT GREEN BEAN AND HAZELNUT SALAD

125g (4 oz) asparagus tips
225g (8 oz) very fresh crisp green beans
30ml (2 tbsp) shelled hazelnuts, sliced

Dressing:
pinch of sugar
2.5ml (¹/₂ tsp) English or Dijon mustard
60ml (4 tbsp) hazelnut oil
1 small clove garlic
salt
squeeze of lemon juice

To make the dressing, in a large bowl, whisk together the sugar, mustard and oil. Add the garlic, salt and lemon juice and continue to whisk until the dressing thickens slightly.

Trim the asparagus and top and tail the beans. Either steam or cook the vegetables in boiling water for a few minutes until just cooked but still crunchy. Quickly refresh in cold water and drain. Immediately add to the dressing with the hazelnuts. Toss and serve immediately, while still crisp, hot and delicious!

MASHED POTATOES WITH CELERIAC

This accompaniment is as straightforward as it sounds.

1kg (2 lb) potatoes
¹/₂ celeriac root
50g (2 oz) butter
15ml (1 tbsp) cream
salt
freshly grated nutmeg

Peel the potatoes and cut into halves or quarters, according to size. Dice the celeriac. Cook the potatoes and celeriac in boiling water until tender. Drain and mash with the butter and cream, seasoning with salt and nutmeg. I prefer not to mash too finely, so that you can 'discover' tiny nuggets of celeriac as you eat.

Pear Clafoutis with Poire Willem Sorbet

You only need half of this quantity of pastry, so freeze the other half for later use.

Pastry:
250g (9 oz) plain flour
25g (1 oz) ground almonds
15ml (1 tbsp) icing sugar
150g (5 oz) unsalted butter, diced
pinch of salt
1 egg yolk
15ml (1 tbsp) cold water
15ml (1 tbsp) rum

Filling and Sorbet:
5 pears (preferably William)
150ml (1/4 pint) water
75 ml (5 tbsp) Poire Willem eau-de-vie or kirsch
40g (1 1/2 oz) caster sugar
1 egg white, beaten
45ml (3 tbsp) vanilla sugar
45ml (3 tbsp) ground almonds
60ml (4 tbsp) double cream
2 eggs, beaten
20g (3/4 oz) butter, softened

To Decorate:
bay leaves

To make the pastry, put the flour, ground almonds, icing sugar, butter and salt into a blender or food processor and work for 15 seconds until the mixture resembles bread-crumbs. Add the egg yolk, water and rum and whizz for the least amount of time it takes to amalgamate the dough and not a second longer. Turn out and knead briefly and lightly. Wrap in cling film and leave to rest in the refrigerator for 2 hours.

Peel the pears, halve lengthwise and remove the cores, retaining the stalks.

In a large pan, heat the water, 60ml (4 tbsp) Poire Williem or kirsch and the caster sugar until dissolved. Add the pears and poach gently until cooked but still firm. Lift out all but one of them, transfer to a plate and allow to cool.

To make the sorbet, purée the remaining pear with the cooking liquor in a blender or food processor. Transfer to a bowl and let cool, then stir in the beaten egg white. Put into a shallow freezerproof container and freeze until firm, whisking from time to time.

Meanwhile, roll out the pastry thinly on a lightly floured surface and use to line 4 individual loose-bottomed flan tins. Slice the pear halves, almost to the stalks, creating little fans. Arrange in the pastry cases with the stalks protruding.

In a bowl, combine the vanilla sugar, ground almonds, remaining 15ml (1 tbsp) Poire Williem or kirsch, the cream ,eggs and butter. Beat thoroughly until you have a rich light batter. Pour into the flan cases and bake in a preheated oven at 200°C (400°F) mark 6 for 20-25 minutes until the topping is a rich golden brown.

Serve the flans on individual plates with a scoop of sorbet. Decorate with bay leaves.

THE FIRST
SEMI-FINAL

AMITA BALDOCK • ANGELA JAQUES • JENNIFER TWYDELL

JENNIFER TWYDELL'S MENU

STARTER
Prawn Brochettes

MAIN COURSE
Duck with Mango
New Potatoes
Selection of Spring Vegetables
Courgette Fritters
"MOIST AND MELTING INSIDE... PERFECT FRITTERS" LOYD

DESSERT
Raspberry Hazelnut Meringue with Framboise Sabayon
"VERY BEAUTIFUL LOOKING SABAYON" LOYD

PRAWN BROCHETTES

16 raw king prawns, shelled
45ml (3 tbsp) olive oil
45ml (3 tbsp) sunflower oil
2 cloves garlic, crushed
15ml (1 tbsp) chopped parsley
salt and freshly ground pepper
50g (2 oz) fine dried breadcrumbs
4 lemon wedges to serve

Mix the prawns with the oils, garlic, parsley, salt and pepper. Add enough breadcrumbs to make a light creamy coating on the prawns. Leave to marinate for at least 20 minutes.

Thread 4 prawns onto each of 4 skewers and place under a pre-heated grill on high for 2-3 minutes each side until golden brown. Serve with lemon wedges.

DUCK WITH MANGO

4 boneless duck breasts
salt and freshly ground white pepper
45ml (3 tbsp) duck stock
30ml (2 tbsp) butter
30ml (2 tbsp) mango chutney
30ml (2 tbsp) orange juice
15ml (1 tbsp) cognac
5ml (1 tsp) potato flour
1 mango, peeled, stoned and sliced

Fry the duck breasts, skin side down, in a hot frying pan until golden brown, about 6 minutes. Turn over, lower the heat slightly and cook until tender. Season with salt and pepper. Remove the duck breasts from the pan and keep warm.

Skim off the duck fat from the juices in the pan. Add the stock to the pan, stirring to deglaze, then add the butter, mango chutney, orange juice and cognac. Heat stirring, to make a sauce. Slake the potato flour with a little water and stir into the sauce to thicken.

Slice the duck and arrange with the sliced mango on warmed serving plates. Pour over the sauce. Serve with courgette fritters, new potatoes and a selection of spring vegetables.

COURGETTE FRITTERS

225g (8 oz) courgettes
60ml (4 tbsp) plain flour
salt and freshly ground pepper
sunflower oil for shallow frying

Cut the courgettes into diagonal 5mm (1/4 inch) slices. Mix the flour with enough water to form a creamy batter. Season with salt and pepper. Pour oil into a large frying pan to a depth of 1cm (1/2 inch) and place over moderate heat. When the oil is hot, dip the courgettes into the batter to coat; then fry, a few at a time, until golden brown, turning as necessary. Drain on kitchen paper, sprinkle with salt and keep warm in the oven while cooking the remainder. Serve immediately.

RASPBERRY HAZELNUT MERINGUE WITH FRAMBOISE SABAYON

Meringue:
2 egg whites
125g (4 oz) caster sugar
2.5ml (1/2 tsp) vinegar
few drops of vanilla essence
50g (2 oz) shelled hazelnuts, toasted and coarsely ground

Filling and Topping:
150ml (1/4 pint) double cream, whipped
175g (6 oz) raspberries (fresh or frozen and thawed)
icing sugar for dusting

Sabayon:
2 egg yolks
25g (1 oz) caster sugar
75ml (3 fl oz) sweet white wine
30ml (2 tbsp) crème de framboise liqueur

To prepare the meringue, line a baking sheet with non-stick paper and draw on 8 circles, 6cm (2½ inches) in diameter. Whisk the egg whites until stiff, then add the sugar a spoonful at a time, beating continuously until the mixture is very stiff. Beat in the vinegar and vanilla essence. Fold in the coarsely ground hazelnuts.

Put the meringue in a nylon piping bag fitted with a 1cm (1½ inch) plain nozzle. Pipe around the outlines, then fill in each circle. Bake in a preheated oven at 170ºC (325ºF) mark 3 for about 25 minutes, until lightly coloured and crisp on the outside, but still soft inside. Leave to cool.

About 30 minutes before serving, sandwich the meringues together in pairs with cream and raspberries.

To make the sabayon, put the egg yolks and sugar into a heatproof bowl and whisk over a pan of very hot water until the sugar is dissolved and the mixture is pale and creamy. Slowly pour in the wine and framboise, whisking continuously. After whisking for about 5 minutes, the mixture should have doubled in volume. Continue whisking until light and foamy. The sabayon may now be served hot, or alternatively cooled over iced water, whisking from time to time, then served cold.

To serve, decorate the meringues with cream and raspberries as desired. Dust with a little icing sugar. Spread a pool of sabayon on each serving plate and carefully place a meringue on the sabayon. Serve immediately.

THE SECOND
SEMI-FINAL

SUE LAWRENCE • ROGER ASHBY • NICOLE SOCHER

WINNER

SUE LAWRENCE'S MENU

STARTER

Fresh Pasta with Chicken Livers and Lemon Sauce

"A PRETTY FAULTLESS CHICKEN LIVER...THAT IS A GREAT DISH" LOYD

MAIN COURSE

Sea Bass with Red Pepper and Basil Sauce, and Tomato Concassé

Seasonal Salad Leaves and Herbs with Balsamic Dressing

Focaccia

"I WOULD SAY 3 ROSETTES" ANTON EDELMANN

DESSERT

Walnut and Quince Tarts served with Quince Cream

"I NEED THE RECIPE FOR THIS" ANTON EDELMAN

FRESH PASTA WITH CHICKEN LIVERS AND LEMON SAUCE

Fresh pasta is at its best when cooked and served immediately after making. It can, however, be left to dry for up to 30 minutes before cooking.

Pasta Dough:
225g (8 oz) strong white flour (preferably Italian wheat flour type oo)
3.75ml (³/₄ tsp) salt
1 egg
1 egg yolk (egg white reserved)
small handful of flat-leaved parsley
small handful of chervil
5ml (1 tsp) white wine
5ml (1 tsp) olive oil

Sauce:
225g (8 oz) chicken livers, trimmed
15ml (1 tbsp) olive oil
250-300ml (8-10 fl oz) homemade chicken stock
2-3 cloves garlic, crushed
25g (1 oz) Parmesan cheese, freshly grated
45-60ml (3-4 tbsp) double cream
strip of finely pared lemon zest, blanched
salt and freshly ground pepper

To Garnish:
flat-leaved parsley and chervil sprigs

To make the pasta dough, put the flour, salt, egg and egg yolk into a food processor and work until evenly mixed. Add the herbs, wine and oil, then process briefly until the dough begins to hold together, adding reserved egg white as necessary to bind. Wrap in cling film and leave to rest in the refrigerator for 30 minutes.

Put the pasta dough through a pasta machine until thin and silky, then cut into tagliatelle. If you do not have a pasta machine, roll out the dough as thinly as possible and cut into long thin strips.

To make the sauce, cut the chicken livers in half. Heat the oil in a large frying pan, add the livers and fry, turning, for 2 minutes. Drain on kitchen paper, then place in a dish and leave to rest in a low oven, set at 150°C (300°F) mark 2, while preparing the sauce.

Pour the stock into the pan and simmer until reduced by about half. Add the garlic, Parmesan, cream and lemon zest; reduce, then add seasoning to taste. Pass through a sieve.

Meanwhile, cook the pasta in boiling salted water until *al dente;* this will take only 30 seconds if cooked immediately; up to 2 minutes if the pasta has been left to dry for a short while. Drain thoroughly.

Arrange the pasta in a twirl on each serving plate. Surround with chicken livers and pour the sauce over them. Serve immediately, garnished with torn parsley and chervil leaves.

SEA BASS WITH RED PEPPER AND BASIL SAUCE, AND TOMATO CONCASSÉ

*4 fillets of sea bass (preferably English),
each about 175g (6 oz)*
olive oil for brushing
salt and freshly ground pepper
small handful of basil leaves

Tomato Concassé:
*225g (8 oz) ripe tomatoes (Italian plum or
beefsteak variety)*
handful of basil leaves, torn

Red Pepper and Basil Sauce:
2 red peppers, halved, cored and seeded
15ml (1 tbsp) extra virgin olive oil
*5ml (1 tsp) chilli-flavoured olive oil
(optional)*
15ml (1 tbsp) chopped shallots
1 clove garlic, crushed
2-3 good handfuls of basil leaves
400ml (14 fl oz) fish stock

Check over the sea bass fillets, tweezing out any small bones and removing any scales. Brush with oil and season with salt and pepper. Slash the skin of each fillet in 2 or 3 places and insert basil leaves in the slits. Cover with oiled cling film and leave to marinate for 1 hour or longer.

To prepare the tomato concassé, skin the tomatoes, then halve and remove the seeds. Finely dice the tomato flesh and add basil and seasoning to taste.

To make the red pepper and basil sauce, roughly chop the peppers. Heat the oils in a pan, add the shallots and garlic and cook gently until softened. Add the red peppers and basil, then add the fish stock and simmer, uncovered, for about 20 minutes. Transfer to a blender or food processor and work to a purée. Pass through a sieve. Check seasoning and keep the sauce warm.

Unwrap the sea bass fillets and cook under a preheated high grill, turning occasionally, for 5-6 minutes, depending on thickness. Transfer to individual plates, surround with the red pepper and basil sauce and top with a spoonful of tomato concassé. Serve immediately.

SEASONAL SALAD LEAVES AND HERBS WITH BALSAMIC DRESSING

selection of salad leaves, i.e. lamb's lettuce, lollo rosso, oakleaf lettuce and watercress
selection of salad herbs, i.e. chervil, dill, sweet cicely, bronze fennel

Dressing:
15ml (1 tbsp) balsamic vinegar
2.5ml (¹/2 tsp) Dijon mustard
coarse sea salt
freshly ground pepper
75ml (5 tbsp) extra virgin olive oil
(approximately)

Combine all the salad leaves in a bowl. Add the herbs, which should be roughly torn if large.

To make the dressing, mix the vinegar with the mustard and seasoning in a small bowl. Whisk in enough olive oil to give a thick emulsion.

Pour the dressing over the salad and toss lightly to serve.

FOCACCIA

For this delicious rosemary-flavoured Italian bread, you really do need to use the right flour. You should be able to buy it from any good Italian delicatessen.

225g (8 oz) strong white flour (Italian wheat flour type oo)
2.5ml (¹/2 tsp) salt
15g (¹/2 oz) fresh yeast
pinch of sugar
150-175ml (5-6 fl oz) lukewarm water
15ml (1 tbsp) olive oil
olive oil for brushing
coarse sea salt
handful of rosemary leaves

To Finish:
rosemary-flavoured olive oil for brushing

Sift the flour and salt into a large bowl. In a small bowl, dissolve the yeast and sugar in 60ml (2 fl oz) of the water. Leave for about 10 minutes until frothy. Pour on to the flour. Mix in the olive oil and enough water to bind to a soft dough. Knead for about 10 minutes, then roll in a little oil and leave to rise in a warm place for about 1 hour.

Knock back the dough, knead briefly and shape into a round, 8mm (³/8 inch) thick. Place on an oiled baking sheet. Press your knuckles into the dough at 5-7.5cm (2-3 inch) intervals to make dimples. Sprinkle liberally with oil and salt, then put a few rosemary leaves in each dimple. Let rise for 15 minutes.

Bake in a preheated oven at 230°C (450°F) mark 8 for about 20 minutes. Brush the focaccia with rosemary oil and serve warm.

WALNUT AND QUINCE TARTS

Make sure you use really fresh walnuts for this tart. My local health food shop sells light amber walnuts, which are ideal.

Rich Shortcrust Pastry:

125g (4 oz) plain flour
pinch of salt
50g (2 oz) caster sugar
50g (2 oz) ground almonds
75g (3 oz) unsalted butter
juice of 1/2 lemon
1 egg

Filling:

3 eggs
50g (2 oz) light muscovado sugar
125g (4 oz) unsalted butter, melted
125g (4 oz) golden syrup
finely grated rind and juice of 1 lemon
225g (8 oz) shelled walnuts

To Glaze:

30ml (2 tbsp) quince jelly
7.5ml (1/2 tbsp) quince eau-de-vie or lemon juice

To make the pastry, sift the flour and salt into the food processor bowl. Add the sugar and ground almonds and process briefly to mix. Add the butter, in pieces, and process until the mixture resembles fine breadcrumbs. Add the lemon juice and egg and process briefly until the dough begins to hold together. Gather the pastry into a ball, wrap in cling film and leave to rest in the refrigerator for 30 minutes or longer.

Roll out the pastry thinly on a lightly floured surface and use to line 4 individual 10cm (4 inch) loose-bottomed flan tins. Line each with a disc of greaseproof paper and baking beans and bake blind at 200°C (400°F) mark 6 for 10 minutes. Remove the paper and beans and bake for a further 5 minutes.

Meanwhile prepare the filling. In a bowl, beat the eggs with the sugar, butter and syrup until smooth. Stir in the lemon rind and juice.

Divide the walnuts between the cooked pastry cases and spoon the filling mixture on top. Bake at 175°C (360°F) mark 3 for 20-25 minutes until set. Gently warm the quince jelly with the eau-de-vie or lemon juice until melted. Brush over the tarts as soon as they are removed from the oven, to glaze. Serve the walnut and quince tarts warm, with quince cream.

QUINCE CREAM

225g (8 oz) mascarpone (Italian soft cream cheese)
25ml (5 tsp) quince jelly
15ml (1 tbsp) quince eau-de-vie (or to taste)

Beat the mascarpone in a bowl until smooth. Gently warm the quince jelly until melted then carefully fold into the mascarpone with the eau-de-vie. Serve at room temperature.

THE SECOND

SEMI-FINAL

SUE LAWRENCE • ROGER ASHBY • NICOLE SOCHER

ROGER ASHBY'S MENU

STARTER

Lobster Tails and Scallops with Saffron Cream Sauce

MAIN COURSE

Fillet of Hare in a Port Sauce with Pears and Blackcurrants
Pot-roasted Baby Potatoes
Kohlrabi
Purple-sprouting Broccoli
Carrots

DESSERT

Mango Tarte Tatin with Passion Fruit Coulis

JO EITEL'S STARTER (SEMI-FINAL)

Mussel Soup with Saffron and Orange

AMITA BALDOCK'S MAIN COURSE (FINAL)

*Calves Liver and Papaya with a Madeira Sauce
Potato Roses*

LOBSTER TAILS AND SCALLOPS WITH SAFFRON CREAM SAUCE

2 small lobsters, each about 225g (8 oz)
bouquet garni
4 scallops, cleaned
2 carrots
2 leeks
1/2 celeriac
600ml (1 pint) fish stock (made from sole bones)
1 glass Noilly Prat
7g (1/4 oz) saffron strands
300ml (1/2 pint) double cream

To Garnish:
chervil leaves

Cook the lobsters in a large pan of boiling water, with the bouquet garni added, for 12 minutes. Drain, rinse in cold water, then allow to cool. Remove the outer membrane from the scallops; set aside the coral for garnish if desired.

Cut the vegetables into julienne strips and blanch them separately in boiling salted water for 2 minutes. Immediately plunge into cold water and drain.

Heat the fish stock and Noilly Prat in a pan and simmer until reduced by half. Add half of the saffron strands. Put the remaining saffron in a small dish and add 125ml (4 fl oz) boiling water; leave to soften, then drain.

Add the cream to the reduced stock and simmer until reduced by half. Add the blanched vegetable julienne and the white scallops. Poach for no longer than 2 minutes, then remove the vegetables and scallops.

Remove the lobster claws, then split the tails down the middle. Discard the black intestinal thread. Slice the lobster meat thinly across the grain. Slice the scallops. If using the scallop coral for garnish, poach for 2 minutes in a little stock.

To assemble, place a small mound of vegetables on each plate and arrange the lobster and scallop slices on top. Spoon over the sauce and garnish with the reserved saffron, chervil and coral if desired.

Note: If the sauce is too thin, whisk in a little butter to thicken.

FILLETS OF HARE IN A PORT SAUCE WITH PEARS AND BLACKCURRANTS

Generally it will be difficult to buy only the best cut from the hare, so be kind to your butcher and purchase the whole animal! Use the remainder for a casserole or game terrine. The tender fillets do not need marinating.

2 fillets of hare, cut from the back, 450g (1 lb) total weight
salt and freshly ground pepper
8 juniper berries
clarified butter for brushing
2 William pears
sugar syrup for poaching
225g (8 oz) blackcurrants
a little sugar
600ml (1 pint) homemade chicken stock
125ml (4 fl oz) port
5ml (1 tsp) blackcurrant preserve (optional)

Skin the fillets, then dust very lightly with salt. Crush the juniper berries and place evenly along each fillet. Brush with clarified butter.

Peel and halve the pears, then poach in sugar syrup until tender. Drain on kitchen paper and allow to cool. Gently heat the blackcurrants with a little sugar until soft, but do not allow to break down. Remove the cores from the pears when cool.

Heat the stock in a pan, add the port and simmer to reduce by half. Check the seasoning. If the sauce needs a lift, add a little blackcurrant preserve.

Cook the hare fillets under a preheated hot grill for 3 minutes each side. Remove, cover with foil and allow to rest for 10 minutes. After resting, the fillets should be pink in the middle. Take care to avoid overcooking hare, otherwise it will be tough and lose its flavour.

To assemble, cut the hare fillets crosswise into 5mm (1/4 inch) slices. Arrange on individual plates. Slice each pear half into a fan leaving it attached at the stalk end. Top with a spoonful of blackcurrants and arrange alongside the hare. Serve with the port sauce, and accompanied by a selection of vegetables, such as kohlrabi, purple-sprouting broccoli, carrots and pot-roasted baby potatoes.

Note: Kohlrabi is an ideal accompaniment because it cuts through the richness of the sauce.

Mango Tarte Tatin with Passion Fruit Coulis

A great combination!

225g (8 oz) sugar
4 ripe mangoes
300g (10 oz) ready-made puff pastry
4 passion fruit
juice of 1/2 lemon

Butter four 12cm (6 inch) flameproof gratin dishes and coat the inside of each with 50g (2 oz) sugar. Peel the mangoes and cut the flesh into slices, discarding the stones. Set aside a quarter of the mango for the coulis; arrange the rest of the slices over the bases of the gratin dishes.

Roll out the pastry on a lightly floured surface to a 3mm (1/8 inch) thickness. Cut out and position lids for the gratin dishes, allowing sufficient pastry to overlap by 2cm (3/4 inch) all the round. Fold back excess pastry. Chill in the refrigerator for 15 minutes.

Place the gratin dishes over a high heat for about 10 minutes to caramelise the sugar; take care to ensure it doesn't burn. Transfer to a preheated oven at 200°C (400°F) mark 6 and bake for about 20 minutes until the pastry is cooked.

To prepare the coulis, halve the passion fruit and scoop out the pulp and seeds into a blender or food processor. Add the reserved mango and lemon juice and work to a purée. Pass through a sieve.

To serve, invert the tarte tatins on to individual plates. Pour the fruit coulis over the caramelised mango topping and serve.

THE SECOND
SEMI-FINAL

SUE LAWRENCE • ROGER ASHBY • NICOLE SOCHOR

NICOLE SOCHOR'S MENU

STARTER
Chilled Watercress and Lime Soup

MAIN COURSE
Moroccan Couscous with Pumpkin

"THIS IS BETTER THAN THE ONE I HAD IN MOROCCO"
ANTON EDELMANN

"THIS IS JUST THE COUSCOUS" LOYD

DESSERT
Orange and Grand Marnier Mousse

CHILLED WATERCRESS AND LIME SOUP

3 shallots
1 small leek (white part only)
1 small potato
15g (¹/₂ oz) unsalted butter
450g (1 lb) watercress
600ml (1 pint) water
60ml (4 tbsp) whipping cream
5ml (1 tsp) lime juice
1/2 lime
pinch of sugar
60ml (4tbsp) crème fraîche
salt

Finely chop the shallots and leek. Cut the potato into tiny cubes. Heat the butter in a pan and sauté the shallots, leek and potato for 4 minutes. Meanwhile trim and finely chop the watercress; reserve some whole leaves for garnish.

Add the water to the sautéed vegetables and bring to the boil. Add the watercress and cook for 8 minutes; don't overcook. Purée the soup in a blender or food processor, then pass through a sieve. Cool, then chill.

Meanwhile, whip the whipping cream and lightly stir in the lime juice.

Peel the lime half, removing all pith, then cut into tiny triangular segments. Place in a bowl with the pinch of sugar. Blanch the reserved watercress leaves in boiling water for 20 seconds. Stir the crème fraîche into the chilled soup and season with salt to taste. Ladle the soup into individual bowls and top with whipped cream. Decorate with lime segments and watercress leaves to serve.

Note: To speed up chilling, I use an ice cream machine.

MOROCCAN COUSCOUS WITH PUMPKIN

This Moroccan dish is traditionally served with harissa sauce - a spicy condiment - available from delicatessens.

700g (1¹/₂ lb) lamb (shoulder and knuckle)
4 large Spanish onions
225g (8 oz) unsalted butter
1 chicken quarter
2.5ml (¹/₂ tsp) turmeric
5ml (1 tsp) ground ginger
2 pinches of saffron
10ml (2 tsp) freshly ground pepper
salt
1.75 litres (3 pints) light lamb stock
450g (1 lb) couscous
425g (15 oz) can chick peas, drained
450g (1 lb) carrots, cut into chunks
700g (1¹/₂ lb) pumpkin, cut into chunks
175g (6 oz) raisins
60ml (4 tbsp) sugar
1 cinnamon stick

To Serve:
dash of rosewater
sprinkling of ground cinnamon
chopped coriander leaves
harissa sauce

Cut the lamb into 4 or 5 steaks. Halve the onions and slice lengthwise. Heat half of the butter in a large heavy-based saucepan or cooking pot. Add the lamb, chicken, onions, turmeric, ginger, saffron, pepper and salt and fry gently for 3-4 minutes, until lightly coloured. Add the stock, bring to the boil and simmer, covered, for 1 hour.

Meanwhile, empty the couscous on to a baking tray. Pour on about 600ml (1 pint) water, then immediately strain off the water. Leave the moistened couscous to swell for 20 minutes, raking it with your fingers after about 10 minutes to separate the grains.

Place a tight-fitting steamer over the stew pan, making sure it stands well clear of the stew. Put the couscous into the steamer, cover and steam over the simmering stew for 20 minutes.

Return the couscous to the baking tray and sprinkle with a cup of cold salted water, containing 5ml (1 tsp) salt. Let swell for 15 minutes, occasionally sifting with your hands to break up any lumps.

In the meantime, rub the chick peas to remove the skins, then add to the stew with the carrots, pumpkin, raisins and sugar. Return to a simmer and cook for at least a further 30 minutes. Replace the couscous in the steamer and steam over the stew for about 30 minutes. A few minutes before the end of the cooking time, add the cinnamon to the stew.

To serve, toss the couscous in the remaining 125g (4oz) butter and stir out any lumps. Sprinkle with rosewater and cinnamon. Spread the couscous on 4 warmed plated, making a well in the centre. Divide the meat into pieces and place in the centre of the plates. Ladle the stew over the meat and couscous and sprinkle with chopped coriander. Serve with harissa sauce.

ORANGE AND GRAND MARNIER MOUSSE

4-6 oranges
3 passion fruit
15g (¹/₂ oz) powdered gelatine (1 sachet)
30-45ml (2-3 tbsp) Grand Marnier
3 egg whites
75g (3 oz) caster sugar
10ml (2 tsp) lemon juice
200ml (7 fl oz) double cream

To Decorate:
orange segments

Cut the tops off 4 oranges, removing about a quarter of each one. Scoop out all of the flesh into a bowl, using a melon baller. Cut a slice off the base of each orange shell, to enable it to stand upright. Set aside the orange shells. Strain the juice from the orange into a measuring jug. Measure 250ml (8 fl oz), adding the juice from the remaining oranges if necessary.

Halve the passion fruit and scoop out the pulp and juice. Press through a sieve into a saucepan and add 150ml (5 fl oz) of the orange juice. Slowly bring to the boil and simmer until reduced by half.

Heat the remaining 100ml (3 fl oz) orange juice separately, sprinkle on the gelatine and stir until dissolved. Add the reduced fruit juice and let cool. Add the Grand Marnier to taste.

In a bowl, whisk the egg whites until stiff. Gradually add the sugar, whisking until stiff peaks form. Beat in the lemon juice.

In a separate bowl, whip the cream until soft peaks form. Fold in the egg whites, then fold in the orange mixture. Pile into the orange shells. Freeze for about 2 hours. Serve decorated with orange segments.

The Third
—————S E M I - F I N A L—————
Jo Eitel • Sarah Beattie • Sue Longden

——————— Winner ———————

Jo Eitel's Menu

Starter
Mussel Soup with Saffron and Orange

Main Course
Roast Fillet of Venison with a Sloe Gin and Bramble Sauce
Carrot Bundles
Celeriac Purée
Dauphinois Potatoes
Steamed Mangetouts
"IT'S A POETIC MIXTURE" MYRTLE ALLEN

Dessert
Scorched Fruits with Crème Grand Marnier
"IT'S VERY DIFFICULT TO IMPROVE ON FRUIT — BUT THAT
CERTAINLY HAS" DAVID BELLAMY

MUSSEL SOUP WITH SAFFRON AND ORANGE

2kg (4 lb) fresh mussels
2 shallots, chopped
1 leek (white part only), chopped
3 parsley sprigs
1 dill sprig
1 bay leaf
250ml (8 fl oz) dry white wine
500ml (16 fl oz) fish stock
250ml (8 fl oz) water
2.5ml ($^1/_2$ tsp) saffron strands
finely pared zest of 1 orange, shredded
50g (2 oz) celery
50g (2 oz) carrot
50g (2 oz) leek
50g (2 oz) butter
30ml (2 tbsp) Noilly Prat
60-75ml (2-3 fl oz) double cream
salt and freshly ground pepper

Scrub the mussels thoroughly in cold water and remove their beards; discard any open mussels. Place the shallots, leek, herbs, wine, fish stock and water in a large saucepan. Add the mussels. Bring to the boil and simmer for 2 minutes. Remove from the heat and discard the bay leaf.

Lift out the mussels and remove them from their shells, discarding the shells. Set aside 16 mussels. Place the rest in a blender or food processor with the cooking liquor and purée until smooth. Pass the soup through a sieve lined with a double layer of muslin into a clean saucepan. Add the saffron and simmer until reduced by a quarter, then lower the heat.

Meanwhile put the shredded orange zest into a pan with 150ml ($^1/_4$ pint) water and bring to the boil. Simmer for 1 minute, then drain and refresh with cold water. Add to the soup.

Cut the celery, leek and carrot into julienne strips. Heat 25g (1oz) butter in a pan, add the vegetable julienne and sweat for 2-3 minutes, then add to the soup.

Stir in the Noilly Prat and remaining butter, then add the cream and check the seasoning before serving.

FILLET OF VENISON WITH A SLOE GIN AND BRAMBLE SAUCE

If possible use a Cabernet Sauvignon for the marinade and sauce.

450g (1 lb) fillet of venison
olive oil for brushing

Marinade:
300ml ($^1/_2$ pint) red wine
30ml (2 tbsp) olive oil
salt and freshly ground pepper

Sauce:
450ml ($^3/_4$ pint) demi glace (see page 49)
75-90ml (5-6 tbsp) blackberry juice
45ml (3 tbsp) red wine
5 juniper berries, crushed
4 pink peppercorns, crushed
45ml (3 tbsp) sloe gin
125g (4 oz) blackberries
knob of butter

Place the venison in a shallow dish. Mix together the ingredients for the marinade and pour over the venison. Leave to marinate for 1½ hours.

Remove the venison from the marinade, pat dry and brush with olive oil. Roast in a preheated oven at 200°C (400°F) mark 6 for 15-20 minutes.

Meanwhile, prepare the sauce. Put the demi glace, blackberry juice, wine, juniper berries and pink peppercorns in a saucepan and bring to the boil. Simmer until reduced by a third; the sauce should be thick enough to coat the back of a spoon. Add the sloe gin and transfer to a bain marie, or a heatproof bowl over a pan of hot but not boiling water. Add the black-berries and leave to cook gently for 10 minutes, then remove with a slotted spoon.

Place a small mound of blackberries in the centre of each plate. Whisk the knob of butter into the sauce and season with salt and pepper to taste. Cut the venison into 3mm (^{1}/8 inch) slices and arrange overlapping around the blackberries. Spoon the sauce over the venison slices and serve immediately, with the vegetables.

CARROT BUNDLES

4-5 medium carrots
4 cherry tomatoes
salt

Cut the carrots into julienne strips, 7.5cm (3 inches) long. Cut a thin slice from the centre of each tomato and gently remove the pulp so that you have a circle of tomato with a hole through the middle.

Carefully slide a small bundle of carrot strips into the tomato ring. The finished effect should look like a tomato napkin ring, with the carrots making up the napkin!

To cook, place the 4 parcels in a steamer over boiling salted water and steam for 3-4 minutes; the carrots should be cooked but slightly firm.

CELERIAC PURÉE

^{1}/2 medium celeriac
25g (1 oz) butter
75ml (5 tbsp) double cream
salt and freshly ground pepper

Cut the celeriac into 2.5cm (1 inch) cubes and place in a saucepan. Cover with cold water and bring to the boil. Simmer for 10-15 minutes until very tender. Drain and purée in a food processor or blender with the butter and cream until very smooth. Add salt and pepper to taste. Serve an oval nugget of celeriac on the side of each dinner plate.

DAUPHINOIS POTATOES

25g (1 oz) butter, melted
1 large clove garlic
150ml (^{1}/4 pint) milk
150ml (^{1}/4 pint) double cream
salt and freshly ground black pepper
4 medium potatoes, peeled

Brush a 12cm (6 inch) round oven-proof dish with half of the melted butter. Rub the garlic clove over the buttered surface, then put the rest of the clove in a saucepan with the milk and cream. Bring to the boil, then remove from the heat and add salt and pepper to taste. Discard the garlic.

Slice the potatoes very thinly, then rinse under cold running water to remove the starch. Drain and pat dry. Place a thin layer of potato in the buttered dish, then pour over a little milk liquid. Repeat until all the potato slices are used. Brush the top with the remaining melted butter. Cook in a preheated oven at 180°C (350°F) mark 4 for 45-55 minutes.

Cut out 4 rounds of dauphinois potatoes, using a 6cm (2^1/2 inch) plain cutter. Serve on one side of each dinner plate.

STEAMED MANGETOUTS

24 mangetouts, trimmed
salt

Place the mangetouts in a steamer over boiling salted water and steam for 1½ minutes. Drain.

To serve, arrange 3 crossed pairs of mangetouts around the edge of each dinner plate.

SCORCHED FRUITS WITH CREME GRAND MARNIER

To scorch the fruits I actually use a blow lamp which is very effective. It quickly caramelises the sugar - scorching the fruit beautifully without cooking it.
Obviously you need to be careful if you use a blow torch in the kitchen.

2 large pears
2 peaches
2 oranges
16 strawberries, hulled
30ml (2 tbsp) Grand Marnier
120ml (8 tbsp) caster sugar

Crème Grand Marnier:
300ml (½ pint) milk
1 vanilla pod, split
2 eggs
15ml (1 tbsp) sugar
45ml (3 tbsp) Grand Marnier
20ml (4 tsp) clear honey, warmed

First prepare the crème Grand Marnier. Put the milk and vanilla pod in a saucepan and bring to just below the boil, then remove from the heat and leave to infuse for 5 minutes. Whisk the eggs, sugar and Grand Marnier together in a bowl, then gradually whisk in the milk.

Spread a teaspoon of honey in the bottom of each of 4 ramekins, then gently pour in the crème Grand Marnier . Bake in a preheated oven at 160ºC (325ºF) mark 3 for 40-45 minutes.

Meanwhile prepare the fruit. Peel the pears, cut in half lengthwise and scoop out the cores. Place flat side down and slice lengthwise from the base, leaving the top half intact. Gently fan out the slices. Immerse the peaches in a bowl of hot water briefly to loosen the skins, then peel. Halve the peaches, remove the stones and slice into 2cm (¾ inch) segments. Peel and segment the oranges, removing all pith.

Place all of the fruits on a metal baking tray, sprinkle with the Grand Marnier and leave for 10 minutes. Sprinkle with caster sugar.

To scorch the fruits, move a blow lamp flame slowly over the fruit until the sugar caramelises and the fruit is scorched. Alternatively place under a preheated very hot grill for about ½ minute.

Arrange the fruit on your dessert plates. I make a flower pattern with the peach slices, a little mountain of strawberries, and so on. Leave the centre of the plate empty for the crème Grand Marnier. Run a knife around the inside of each ramekin and turn out a custard into the centre of each dessert plate. Serve immediately.

THE THIRD
SEMI-FINAL
JO EITEL • SARAH BEATTIE • SUE LONGDEN

SARAH BEATTIE'S MENU

STARTER
Tomato and Stilton Ice Cream

MAIN COURSE
Kohlrabi en Cage with Oyster Mushrooms
Glazed Carrots
Braised Leeks
Lemony Potatoes

DESSERT
Caramelised Pear and Ginger Puddings
Crème Anglaise

TOMATO AND STILTON ICE CREAM

A pretty pinky-red ice cream that has people asking "Wow, what's that?!" Serve in cucumber cups, or tomato cups or on a bed of green salad leaves.

450g (1 lb) good red tomatoes, roughly chopped
juice of 1 lemon
15-30ml (1-2 tbsp) vodka
pinch of sugar
pinch of cayenne pepper
coarse sea salt
freshly ground black pepper
2 free-range eggs, separated
125g (4 oz) Stilton cheese
300ml (¹/₂ pint) double cream

Put the chopped tomatoes, including the skin, tops and seeds, into a pan with the lemon juice and cook until soft and pulpy. Press through a sieve into a clean pan. Stir in the vodka and add sugar, cayenne, salt and pepper to taste. Beat in the egg yolks and cook over a low heat until the mixture thickens, stirring constantly.

Remove from the heat and crumble in the Stilton, stirring well until it melts into the mixture. Leave to cool.

Whip the cream until it just holds its shape. Fold into the Stilton and tomato mixture. Whisk the egg whites until they form soft peaks, then fold into the mixture. Transfer to a shallow freezerproof container and freeze until mushy.

Turn into a bowl and beat well. Return to the freezer and freeze until almost firm, then beat again. Either freeze in moulds or in a covered container. Allow to soften slightly before serving.

KOHLRABI EN CAGE WITH OYSTER MUSHROOMS

Cups of kohlrabi cradle a filling of oyster mushrooms, garlic and shallots, cooked in olive oil and flavoured with lemon thyme. A portcullis of egg-glazed pastry covers the whole. The accompanying vegetables are baby carrots, baked in honey and orange, and braised leeks.

4 kohlrabi
125g (4 oz) shallots
4 cloves garlic
a little olive oil
225g (8 oz) oyster mushrooms
finely chopped lemon thyme leaves to taste
2 hard-boiled eggs
salt and freshly ground pepper

Shortcrust Pastry:
350g (12 oz) plain unbleached flour
75g (3 oz) unsalted butter
75g(3 oz) solid vegetable oil
a little water to bind

To Glaze:
1 egg yolk, beaten with a little water

Peel the kohlrabi, halve crosswise and par-boil in boiling salted water until just tender; drain and scoop out the centres to leave cups.

Meanwhile, make the pastry. Sift the flour into a bowl. Rub the fat into the flour, then add a little water to bind the pastry. Knead only lightly to bring the dough together, then wrap in cling film and chill.

To make the filling, finely chop the shallots and garlic and cook gently in a little olive oil until softened. Shred the oyster mushrooms and add to the pan with very finely chopped lemon thyme and salt and pepper to taste. Cook over a low heat until the mushrooms are tender. Chop the hard-boiled eggs and add to the pan, stirring well. Check the seasoning. Spoon a generous helping of filling into each kohlrabi cup, pressing well down and rounding the tops.

Roll out the pastry thinly on a lightly floured surface. Cut out eight 15cm (6 inch) circles and slash each to form a lattice pattern, leaving an uncut margin of 1cm (1/2 inch) around the edge. Gently easing the cuts open, lift over the kohlrabi filling and wrap the pastry around the bottom of the cups. Place on a baking sheet and brush with egg glaze. Bake in a pre-heated oven at 190ºC (375ºF) mark 5 for 20 minutes or until golden. Serve immediately, with accompaniments.

GLAZED CARROTS

The preparation of the carrots depends on their size. Baby carrots should merely be scrubbed and carefully trimmed. Larger ones should be cut into bâtons. The texture and colour of the carrots is preserved, and the honey and orange bring out their natural sweetness.

450g (1 lb) baby carrots
1 large (unwaxed) sweet orange
25g (1 oz) unsalted butter
30ml (2 tbsp) heather honey

Scrub and trim the carrots, chiselling the rounded ends. Place in a small buttered casserole dish. Finely grate a little orange rind over the carrots. Squeeze over the juice from the orange. Drizzle with honey and dot with the remaining butter. Cover and cook in a preheated oven at 190ºC (375ºF) mark 5 for 30 minutes or until tender. Spoon the glaze over the carrots, before serving.

LEMONY POTATOES

Best made with small rather waxy new potatoes, this is an exciting change from the minted potatoes we are so familiar with.

450g (1 lb) small new potatoes, i.e. Jersey Royals
1 lemon
30ml (2 tbsp) soft white breadcrumbs
freshly ground black pepper
coarse sea salt
25g (1 oz) unsalted butter

Scrape or scrub the potatoes and par-boil until just tender. Drain and place in an ovenproof dish. Grate the lemon rind and mix into the breadcrumbs with plenty of freshly ground pepper and a little salt. Squeeze the lemon and sprinkle the juice over the potatoes. Scatter the breadcrumb mixture over the top and dot with small pieces of butter. Bake in a preheated oven at 200ºC (400ºF) mark 6 for 10-15 minutes.

CARAMELISED PEAR AND GINGER PUDDINGS

An old fashioned sponge pudding with a dark fruity topping, served with a proper crème anglaise. Made in ramekins to be turned out on to individual plates, this is a warming and comforting pudding.

Pear and Ginger Pudding:
butter for greasing
dark muscovado sugar for coating
4 pears, preferably firm Conference
4 pieces of crystallised ginger
50g (2 oz) unsalted butter
50g (2 oz) soft brown sugar
1 free-range egg, beaten
50g (2 oz) self-raising flour

Crème Anglaise:
300ml (1/2 pint) double cream
1 vanilla pod, split
2 free-range eggs
30-60ml (2-4 tbsp) caster sugar

Grease 4 ramekins thoroughly with butter. Sprinkle the insides liberally with muscovado sugar to coat well. Peel, core and thinly slice the pears. Arrange in overlapping slices over the base and sides of the ramekins. Place a nugget of crystallised ginger in the centre.

Beat the butter until light, then beat in the soft brown sugar. Gradually beat in the egg. Lightly fold in the flour, then spoon the mixture over the pears. Stand the ramekins in a roasting tin containing 2.5cm (1 inch) depth of water. Bake in a preheated oven at 180°C (350°F) mark 4 for 20 minutes.

Meanwhile, prepare the crème anglaise. Put the cream and split vanilla pod in a saucepan and heat gently to just below simmering point. Beat the eggs with the sugar until light and creamy. Pour on the hot cream, beating constantly. Strain into a double boiler or a heatproof bowl over a pan of simmering water and cook, stirring, until the custard is thick enough to coat the back of a spoon.

Allow the puddings to stand for 3-5 minutes, then run a knife around the inside of each dish and turn out on to individual plates. Serve in a pool of crème anglaise.

THE THIRD
——— S E M I - F I N A L ———
JO EITEL • SARAH BEATTIE • SUE LONGDEN

SUE LONGDEN'S MENU

STARTER
*Blinis with Soured Cream, Apples, Frazzled Tomatoes and
Pickled Herrings*
"EVERY PART OF THE TONGUE, A DIFFERENT TASTE...ABSOLUTELY
AMAZING" DAVID BELLAMY

MAIN COURSE
*Caramelised Breast of Barbary Duck with Lavender Honey
Saffron Vegetables*

DESSERT
Serpent Cake with Oranges and Coconut Cream
"I SHOULD THINK IF YOU WERE CLIMBING MOUNT EVEREST, YOU'D
PROBABLY WANT THAT IN YOUR KNAPSACK" LOYD

BLINIS WITH SOURED CREAM, APPLES, FRAZZLED TOMATOES AND PICKLED HERRINGS

Blinis are Russian yeast pancakes, traditionally served with sour cream and caviar. I think my version is even more scrumptious! If preferred, you can serve the topping ingredients separately for your guests to apply their own.

Blinis:

125g (4 oz) plain flour
pinch of salt
7g (1/4 oz) fresh yeast
pinch of sugar
100ml (3 1/2 fl oz) warm water
1 egg, separated
a little oil for frying

Topping:

8 sun-dried tomatoes
1 crisp green apple
150ml (1/4 pint) soured cream
2-3 pickled herrings (preferably homemade), chopped
2 spring onions, finely chopped

To Garnish:

lemon slices
caviar (optional)

For the blinis, sift the flour and salt into a bowl. Crumble the yeast and sugar into a small bowl, mix in the warm water and leave for 5 minutes until creamy and frothy. Beat in the egg yolk. Add to the flour and beat until smooth and creamy. Leave in a warm place for about 1 hour until at least doubled in bulk. Beat the mixture down using a whisk. Whip the egg white until soft peaks form, then fold into the batter. Leave to rest for 20 minutes, or so.

To prepare the frazzled tomatoes for the topping, put the sun-dried tomatoes in a dish, cover with boiling water and leave to rehydrate for a few minutes. Remove, dry and cut into strips. Fry in oil until dark and crispy; they look burnt but taste delicious!

Oil a heavy-based frying pan or griddle and place over a medium heat. When the pan is hot, drop in tablespoons of batter, spacing well apart. Cook for 2-3 minutes on each side, then remove. The blinis may be served hot or cold.

Peel, core and dice the apple into 5mm (1/4 inch) pieces. Fold into the soured cream and spread a spoonful on each blini. Arrange the frazzled tomatoes, herrings and spring onions decoratively on top. Garnish with lemon and caviar if desired.

Note: If serving the blinis hot, wrap them in foil and place in a cool oven to keep warm.

CARAMELISED BREAST OF BARBARY DUCK WITH LAVENDER HONEY

Although the list of ingredients for this main course seems quite daunting, it is actually very simple to prepare and tastes wonderful.

4 Barbary duck breasts, each about 150g (5 oz)

Marinade:

45ml (3 tbsp) honey
5ml (1 tsp) coriander seeds, crushed
5ml (1 tsp) each chopped rosemary, thyme and coriander leaves
60ml (4 tbsp) soy sauce
4 cloves garlic, thinly sliced
5ml (1 tsp) Chinese five-spice powder
pinch of ground cinnamon

Glaze:

45ml (3 tbsp) honey
1-3 stalks lavender (depending on size)
5ml (1 tsp) coriander seeds, crushed
5ml (1 tsp) freshly ground black pepper
5ml (1 tsp) fennel seeds
5ml (1 tsp) finely chopped fresh root
ginger

Sauce:

50g (2 oz) butter
50g (2 oz) shallots, finely chopped
150ml ($^1/_4$ pint) ruby port
150ml ($^1/_4$ pint) red wine
300ml ($^1/_2$ pint) duck stock
15ml (1 tbsp) tomato purée
2.5ml ($^1/_2$ tsp) fennel seeds
2.5ml ($^1/_2$ tsp) coriander seeds, crushed
2.5ml ($^1/_2$ tsp) freshly ground black
pepper
1 bay leaf
1-3 stalks lavender
2.5ml ($^1/_2$ tsp) finely chopped fresh root
ginger
30ml (2 tbsp) honey
juice of 1 lime
pinch of Chinese five-spice powder
dash of balsamic vinegar
salt

To Garnish:

lime slices
star anise

Place the duck breasts in a single layer in a shallow dish. Combine all the ingredients for the marinade, pour over the duck breasts, turn to coat and leave to marinate for several hours or overnight.

Remove the duck from the marinade. Heat a heavy-based frying pan and add the duck breasts, fat-side down. Fry slowly for 10 minutes or until medium rare, turning halfway through cooking. Combine the ingredients for the glaze and add to the pan. Cook gently, turning the duck breasts in the mixture, until evenly glazed. Keep warm.

For the sauce, melt half the butter in a pan and sauté the shallots until softened. Deglaze the pan with the port and wine. Add the stock and tomato purée and reduce by fast boiling to half the original volume. Add the fennel and coriander seeds, pepper, bay leaf, lavender and ginger. Simmer for 5 minutes.

Meanwhile, heat the honey and lime juice together until slightly caramelised. Add to the sauce, then pass through a fine sieve. Return the sauce to a clean saucepan and reheat gently. Stir in the five-spice powder, balsamic vinegar and seasoning to taste. Whisk in the remaining 25g (1 oz) butter, a little at a time, to give a glossy finish.

To serve, cut the duck breasts into thin slices and arrange on warmed serving plates. Spoon over the sauce and garnish with lime slices and star anise. Serve immediately, accompanied by the saffron vegetables.

SAFFRON VEGETABLES

This dish may be prepared in advance and reheated before serving.

pinch of saffron strands
450-750g (1-1$^1/_2$ lb) large potatoes,
peeled
4 large carrots
large knob of butter
2 shallots, finely chopped
1 thyme sprig
1 bay leaf
salt and freshly ground pepper
100ml (3$^1/_2$ fl oz) chicken stock or water

Soak the saffron strands in a little hot water.

Using an apple corer, shape cylinders of potato and carrot. Trim them all to the same length, about 2.5-4cm (1-1¹/2 inches).

Heat the butter in a pan, add the potatoes, carrots and shallots and sweat for 1-2 minutes. Add the saffron, thyme and bay leaf. Season with salt and pepper. Add the stock, cover the pan with buttered paper and simmer for about 15 minutes. Remove the paper and boil to reduce the liquid until the vegetables are glazed. Discard the thyme and bay leaf before serving.

SERPENT CAKE WITH ORANGES AND COCONUT CREAM

This delicious cake can be served warm or cold.

Cake:
2 large sheets of filo pastry
1 egg
icing sugar for dredging
ground cinnamon for dusting

Filling:
225g (8 oz) ground almonds
125g (4 oz) icing sugar
30ml (2 tbsp) orange flower water
15ml (1 tbsp) water
60-90ml (4-6 tbsp) melted butter, cooled
2.5ml (¹/2 tsp) almond essence
2.5ml (¹/2 tsp) vanilla essence
finely grated rind of ¹/2 orange (optional)

Oranges:
2 large oranges (preferably blood oranges)
few drops of orange flower water

Coconut Cream:
25-50g (1-2 oz) creamed coconut
150ml (1/4 pint) double cream
Cointreau to taste

To make the cake filling, combine the ground almonds, icing sugar, orange flower water, water and cooled melted butter. Add the almond and vanilla essences and, if desired, the finely grated orange zest. Mix well, knead to a smooth paste, then chill.

Divide the chilled almond paste into 4 pieces and roll out each piece to a long sausage, 1cm (¹/2 inch) in diameter.

Cut each sheet of filo pastry in half lengthwise. Lay out one pastry strip and place a filling 'sausage' along the bottom long edge. Roll up tightly. Repeat with the remaining filo and 'sausages'.

Line a baking sheet with non-stick paper. Starting at the centre of the baking sheet, arrange the filo-covered 'sausages' in a tight spiral to resemble a coiled snake.

Brush with beaten egg and bake in a preheated oven at 180°C (350°F) mark 4 for about 10 minutes until the pastry is crisp and golden. Turn the filo cake over and bake for a further 10 minutes until the top is crisp and golden.

Transfer to a wire rack, dredge with icing sugar and decorate with fine lines of cinnamon.

Peel and carefully segment the oranges, over a bowl to catch the juice. Add a few drops of orange flower water and chill thoroughly.

Heat the coconut cream very gently until melted, adding a little water if necesary. Stir in the double cream and Cointreau to taste. Mix well; cool. The mixture may seem a bit sloppy at this stage but it will thicken on cooling.

To serve, slice the serpent cake and place a slice on each plate. Add a fan of orange segments and a dollop of coconut cream.

THE
FINAL

SUE LAWRENCE • AMITA BALDOCK • JO EITEL

WINNER

SUE LAWRENCE'S FINAL MENU

STARTER

*Buckwheat Pancakes with Smoked Salmon and Horseradish
Cream*

MAIN COURSE

Noisettes of Lamb with Thyme and Red Wine

Rösti of Pasta

Spinach with Nutmeg

*"IT'S VERY GOOD THAT SPINACH INDEED, I'LL HAVE TO HAVE
SOME MORE OF THAT" LOYD*

DESSERT

Bitter Chocolate Marquise with Cloudberry Sauce

*"I THINK EVERYBODY WOULD CLAP IF THAT WAS PRESENTED TO THEM"
SIR TERENCE CONRAN*

BUCKWHEAT PANCAKES WITH SMOKED SALMON AND HORSERADISH CREAM

Ideally you need a piece of smoked salmon which you can slice obliquely (rather than pre-packed thin slices) for these pancakes.

Pancakes:
150ml (¹/₄ pint) milk
75ml (5 tbsp) water
2.5ml (¹/₂ tsp) caster sugar
15g (¹/₂ oz) butter
125g (4 oz) plain flour
50g (2 oz) buckwheat flour
1.25ml (¹/₄ tsp) salt
1 egg, separated

Topping:
50-75g (2-3 oz) piece smoked salmon fillet, diagonally sliced
5-10ml (1-2 tsp) freshly grated horseradish (or creamed horseradish)
150ml (¹/₄ pint) soured cream

To Garnish:
snipped chives

To make the pancakes, put the milk, water, sugar and butter in a saucepan and heat gently until melted. Pour into a food processor and add the plain and buckwheat flours, salt and egg yolk. Blend to a smooth batter. Transfer to a bowl, cover and leave in a warm place for 1-1¹/₂ hours until frothy. Whisk the egg white until soft peaks form and fold into the batter.

To cook the pancakes, heat a griddle or heavy-based frying pan until very hot. Grease with butter or oil and drop dessertspoonfuls of batter into the pan, spacing well apart. Cook for 1-2 minutes, then place a piece of smoked salmon in the centre of each one. Flip over and cook until the underside is golden brown. Wrap the pancakes loosely in a greased foil parcel and keep warm in a low oven, while cooking the remainder.

Mix the horseradish with the soured cream and serve as a topping for the pancakes. Garnish with chives.

NOISETTES OF LAMB WITH THYME AND RED WINE

2 lamb fillets, each about 225-300g (8-10 oz)
hazelnut oil for brushing
handful of thyme sprigs
25g (1 oz) butter
30ml (2 tbsp) olive oil
salt and freshly ground pepper
150ml (¹/₄ pint) good red wine
300ml (¹/₂ pint) strong lamb stock

Rub the lamb fillets with hazelnut oil and thyme. Place in a shallow dish, cover and leave to marinate for 1-2 hours.

Heat half of the butter and the olive oil in a heavy-based frying pan. Lightly season the lamb and fry, turning frequently, for 5-6 minutes depending on thickness. Remove from the pan and leave to rest in a low oven while making the sauce.

Add the red wine to the pan with a few thyme sprigs, stirring to deglaze. Add the lamb stock and reduce until syrupy. Stir in the remaining butter and check the seasoning. Strain through a muslin-lined sieve.

To serve, cut the lamb into noisettes; they should be pink inside. Arrange on individual serving plates with the rösti of pasta. Spoon the sauce around the noisettes. Serve accompanied by the spinach with nutmeg.

RÖSTI OF PASTA

Pasta Dough:
225g (8 oz) strong white flour (preferably Italian wheat flour type oo)
3.75ml (³/4 tsp) salt
1 egg
1 egg yolk (egg white reserved)
7.5ml (¹/2 tbsp) thyme leaves
5ml (1 tsp) white wine
5ml (1 tsp) olive oil

To Cook Rösti:
olive oil
salt and freshly ground black pepper

To make the pasta dough, put the flour, salt, egg, egg yolk and thyme into a food processor and work until evenly mixed. Add the wine and oil, then process briefly until the dough begins to hold together, adding reserved egg white as necessary to bind. Wrap in cling film and leave to rest in the refrigerator for 30 minutes.

Put the pasta dough through a pasta machine until thin and silky, then cut into spaghetti. If you do not have a pasta machine, roll out the dough as thinly as possible and cut into long fine strips. Cook in boiling water for 30 seconds. Drain well and toss in 5ml (1 tsp) olive oil and seasoning to taste.

Position four 10cm (4 inch) metal rings in a heavy-based frying pan. Add a little olive oil to each ring and heat. When very hot, divide the pasta between the rings, flattening to form nests. Cook for about 2 minutes, then remove the rings and turn the rösti over. Cook until the underside is crisp and golden brown. Drain on kitchen paper.

SPINACH WITH NUTMEG

450g (1 lb) young spinach leaves
7.5ml (¹/2 tbsp) hazelnut oil
7.5ml (¹/2 tbsp) olive oil
15g (¹/2 oz) shallot, finely chopped
2 cloves garlic, crushed
freshly grated nutmeg
coarse sea salt
freshly ground pepper

Roughly tear the spinach leaves. Heat the hazelnut and olive oils in a pan, add the shallot and garlic and sweat for about 2 minutes. Add the torn spinach leaves, with just the water clinging to their leaves after washing. Sauté briefly for about 2 minutes, then season liberally with nutmeg, salt and pepper. Serve immediately.

BITTER CHOCOLATE MARQUISE WITH CLOUDBERRY SAUCE

I usually serve this irresistible rich dessert with raspberry sauce - made from flavourful Scottish raspberries. If you are lucky enough to find cloudberries, do use them; otherwise raspberries make a perfectly good substitute.

200g (7 oz) quality bitter chocolate (Valrhona)
15ml (1 tbsp) strong black coffee
30-45ml (2-3 tbsp) cloudberry liqueur, or framboise eau-de-vie
125g (4 oz) unsalted butter, softened
125g (4 oz) caster sugar
30ml (2 tbsp) cocoa powder
3 egg yolks
300ml (1/2 pint) double cream

Cloudberry Sauce:
450g (1 lb) cloudberries
15ml (1 tbsp) cloudberry liqueur, or framboise eau-de-vie
125-175g (4-6 oz) caster sugar (to taste)

To Decorate:
handful of cloudberries

Break the chocolate into a heatproof bowl and add the coffee and liqueur. Place over a pan of hot water until melted. Allow to cool.

In a bowl, beat the butter with half of the sugar until light and fluffy. Fold in the cocoa powder. In another bowl, whisk the egg yolks with the remaining sugar until pale. Lightly whip the cream.

Beat the cooled chocolate into the butter and cocoa mixture, then stir into the beaten egg yolk mixture. Lightly fold in the cream.

Line 4 small ramekins with cling film. Pour in the chocolate mixture and tap the ramekins to level. Cover and chill for 1 1/2-2 hours until set.

Meanwhile, prepare the cloudberry sauce. Purée the cloudberries with the liqueur and sugar to taste in a blender or food processor. Sieve to remove all the pips.

To serve, invert the marquise on to individual plates, covered with a pool of cloudberry sauce. Cut out a tiny wedge of each marquise to reveal the texture. Decorate with a few fresh cloudberries.

THE

FINAL

SUE LAWRENCE • AMITA BALDOCK • JO EITEL

AMITA BALDOCK'S FINAL MENU

STARTER
Crab and Ginger Wontons with a Citrus Sauce

MAIN COURSE
Calves Liver and Papaya with a Madeira Sauce
Potato Roses
Mixed Leaf and Walnut Salad

DESSERT
Chilled Zabaglione with a hint of Orange
Sponge Biscuits
"IT'S AWFULLY GOOD THAT...PACKS A BIT OF PUNCH AS
WELL ACTUALLY" LOYD

CRAB AND GINGER WONTONS WITH A CITRUS SAUCE

Wonton skins are available fresh or frozen from Oriental food stores and supermarkets. They are approximately 7.5cm (3 inches) square.

12 wonton skins

Filling:
75g (3 oz) Dover sole fillet, skinned
1 egg
60ml (2 fl oz) double cream
175g (6 oz) white crabmeat
7.5ml (1¹/2 tsp) grated fresh root ginger
7.5ml (1¹/2 tsp) light soy sauce
5ml (1 tsp) rice wine
15ml (1 tbsp) finely chopped coriander leaves
2.5ml (¹/2 tsp) sugar
salt and freshly ground pepper

Citrus Sauce:
300ml (¹/2 pint) fish stock
1 pink grapefruit, segmented
juice of 1 lemon
1.25ml (¹/4 tsp) Dijon mustard
2 thin slices fresh root ginger
30ml (2 tbsp) double cream
50g (2 oz) unsalted butter, chilled

To Garnish:
tomato concassé (see note)
coriander leaves

Place the Dover sole, egg and cream in a food processor or blender and process for about 1 minute. Transfer to a bowl, add the remaining filling ingredients and mix thoroughly by hand. Check the seasoning.

Place a generous spoonful of the filling in the middle of each wonton skin. Bring up the sides of the wonton skin and press them down over the top of the filling. Tap the wonton on the bottom to make a flat base. The top should be wide open, exposing the filling. Put the wontons on a heatproof plate and cook in a steamer for 20-25 minutes.

Meanwhile, make the citrus sauce. Bring the fish stock to the boil, then add the grapefruit segments, lemon juice, mustard and ginger. Boil the sauce until it has reduced and the grapefruit segments have broken up. Press through a sieve, then add the double cream. Whisk in the butter, a little at a time, over a low heat. Adjust the seasoning.

To serve, pour a pool of sauce on to each serving plate. Position 3 wontons on each pool of sauce, with a little tomato concassé in the centre. Scatter coriander leaves between the wontons. Serve immediately.

Note: For the tomato concassé, simply peel and seed a few tomatoes, then finely chop the flesh.

CALVES LIVER AND PAPAYA WITH A MADEIRA SAUCE

4 thin slices calves liver, each about
75-125g (3-4 oz)
15ml (1tbsp) flour
salt and freshly ground pepper
50g (2 oz) clarified butter
25g (1 oz) shallots, finely chopped
150ml (¹/4 pint) medium dry Madeira
150ml (¹/4 pint) veal stock
50g (2 oz) unsalted butter, chilled
1 papaya, thinly sliced

Coat the liver lightly with flour and seasoning. Heat the clarified butter in a frying pan. When it is very hot, add the calves liver and cook over a high heat for 1 minute on each side. Transfer to a plate and keep warm.

Sauté the shallots in the same pan until soft, then add the Madeira and boil until reduced by half. Add the stock and boil until the sauce is a little syrupy. Pass the sauce through a sieve into a clean pan and whisk in the chilled butter, a little at a time, over a low heat. Season to taste.

Place the calves liver on individual plates and pour over the sauce. Arrange the papaya slices around the liver and serve immediately, garnished with the potato roses, and accompanied by the mixed leaf and walnut salad.

POTATO ROSES

4 small desirée potatoes, peeled
salt and freshly ground pepper
olive oil for basting

Using a very sharp knife, pare a long thin layer from each potato, from the top winding around to the bottom in one piece, as though you were peeling an apple. Do not break the strip.

Sprinkle each potato with salt and pepper, then roll into a coil to form a rose. Spear the base with a wooden cocktail stick to hold it together.

Liberally oil a baking tray with olive oil and place in a preheated oven at 200°C (400°F) mark 6. Place the potato roses on the hot baking tray and spoon over the hot oil. Bake in the oven, basting with the hot oil every 10 minutes or so, for about 45 minutes or until the roses are crisp and golden. Remove the cocktail sticks and serve the potato roses as a garnish.

MIXED LEAF AND WALNUT SALAD

200g (7 oz) mixed salad leaves, eg
radicchio, endive, sorrel, lollo rosso, frisée,
oakleaf, lamb's lettuce, watercress
50g (2 oz) shelled walnuts

Dressing:
10ml (2 tsp) sherry vinegar
10ml (2 tsp) balsamic vinegar
45ml (3 tbsp) walnut oil
10ml (2 tsp) olive oil
2.5ml (¹/2 tsp) Dijon mustard
¹/2 clove garlic, crushed
salt and freshly ground pepper

Put the salad leaves in a bowl. Briefly immerse the walnuts in boiling water to remove the skins, then drain and pat dry. Break into small pieces and add to the salad leaves.

Put the vinegar, oil, mustard, garlic, salt and pepper in a screw-top jar and shake vigorously to combine.

Pour the dressing over the salad and toss to mix. Divide between individual plates to serve.

CHILLED ZABAGLIONE WITH A HINT OF ORANGE

4 egg yolks
50g (2 oz) caster sugar
150ml ($^1/_4$ pint) Marsala
30ml (2 tbsp) Cointreau, Grand Marnier or other orange liqueur
finely pared strip of orange zest
90ml (6 tbsp) double cream, lightly whipped

Whisk the egg yolks and sugar in a bowl until pale and frothy. Whisk in the Marsala and orange liqueur. Add the orange zest.

Place the bowl over a saucepan of simmering water and whisk the mixture, using a balloon whisk, for 10-15 minutes until thickened. Remove the bowl from the heat and cool slightly, whisking occasionally. Discard zest.

Fold the cream into the slightly cooled zabaglione and pour into individual glasses. Chill before serving, with sponge biscuits.

SPONGE BISCUITS

3 eggs, separated
100g (3$^1/_2$ oz) caster sugar
125g (4 oz) plain flour, sifted
icing sugar for dusting

Whisk the egg yolks with three quarters of the sugar until the mixture is pale and thick enough to leave a trail when the whisk is lifted.

In another bowl, whisk the egg whites until stiff peaks form. Add the remaining sugar and beat for 1 minute at high speed until very stiff.

Using a flat slotted spoon, stir a third of the whisked egg whites into the yolk mixture, then lightly fold in the rest; before the mixture is thoroughly blended, sprinkle the flour over the top and fold in lightly until evenly blended.

Line a baking sheet with buttered greaseproof paper and sprinkle lightly with flour. Pipe sponge fingers on to the paper, about 10cm (4 inches) long and spaced well apart. Lightly dust with icing sugar; leave for 5 minutes then dust again.

Bake in a preheated oven at 190°C (375°F) mark 5 for 10-12 minutes. Allow to cool slightly on the baking sheet, then carefully lift off and transfer to a wire rack. Leave to cool completely.

The
FINAL

Sue Lawrence • Amita Baldock • Jo Eitel

Jo Eitel's Final Menu

Starter

*John Dory and Chicory in a Paper Parcel, served with a
Cardamom Sauce*

"She's got the consistency of the sauce, which is
remarkable — many professional chefs fail" Albert Roux

Main Course

*Wild Boar in a Prune and Brandy Sauce
Steamed Baby Carrots
Roast Parsnips, Potatoes and Chestnuts*

Dessert

Pear Gratin with Cinnamon Ice Cream

"An invitation to sit down and have a good meal"
Albert Roux

JOHN DORY AND CHICORY IN A PAPER PARCEL, WITH A CARDAMON SAUCE

1 small to medium John Dory, filleted and skinned

Fish Stock:
head and bones from the John Dory
2 shallots
1 medium leek (white part only), chopped
2 carrots, finely chopped
1/2 medium fennel bulb, finely chopped
2 parsley sprigs
1 dill sprig
1 thyme sprig
2 sticks celery, finely chopped
1.2 litres (2 pints) water

Sauce:
300ml (1/2 pint) dry white wine
15ml (1 tbsp) cracked cardamom pods
7.5ml (1/2 tbsp) Noilly Prat
50g (2 oz) butter
salt and freshly ground pepper

Parcels:
20ml (4 tsp) olive oil
juice of 1 lemon
salt
1 head of chicory, quartered lengthwise
20 white peppercorns
20 coriander seeds
4 cardamom pods, cracked
4 rosemary sprigs
4 knobs of butter

To prepare the fish stock, place all the ingredients in a saucepan. Bring to the boil, then cover and simmer until the chopped vegetables are tender; pass through a sieve. Measure 1.2 litres (2 pints) fish stock for the sauce.

To make the sauce, place the fish stock, wine and cardamom pods in a saucepan; bring to the boil. Lower the heat and gently reduce the stock to 200ml (7 fl oz). Liquidise in a blender or food processor, then strain into a clean saucepan, saving the cardamom pods; add these to the sauce. Add the Noilly Prat.

To prepare the parcels you will need four 30cm (12 inch) squares of greaseproof paper. To prepare each parcel, brush the centre 12 cm (5 inch) square with olive oil. Fold the greaseproof paper in half and then open out. Just above the fold, place one half fillet of John Dory and sprinkle with lemon juice and a little salt. Beside it, place the chicory, 5 peppercorns, 5 corianders seeds, 1 cardamom pod and a sprig of rosemary. Top with a knob of butter. Refold the greaseproof paper over these ingredients to enclose. Working from the side of the parcel, begin to fold the edges over themselves until you have created a half-circle shaped parcel (following the diagrams below and overleaf).

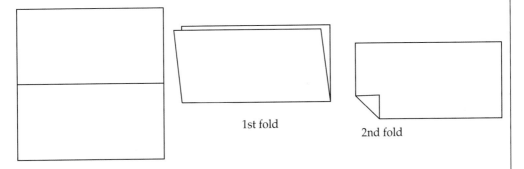

1st fold   2nd fold

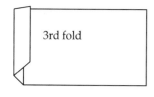

3rd fold

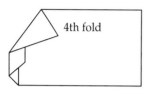

4th fold

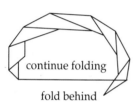

continue folding

fold behind

Cook the parcels in a preheated oven at 200°C (400°F) mark 6 for 10-15 minutes. Just before serving, stir the butter into the sauce and check the seasoning. To serve, place the parcels on individual plates and spoon a little sauce alongside.

WILD BOAR WITH A PRUNE AND BRANDY SAUCE

450g (1 lb) fillet of wild boar

Marinade:
30ml (2 tbsp) rosemary leaves
finely shredded zest of 1 large orange
10ml (2 tsp) crushed bay leaves
1 large garlic clove, crushed
45-60ml (3-4 tbsp) olive oil
15ml (1 tbsp) brandy
salt and freshly ground pepper

Sauce:
450ml (³/₄ pint) demi glace (see page 49)
45ml (3 tbsp) prune juice
30ml (2 tbsp) brandy
16 prunes (no-soak variety)
knob of butter

Place the wild boar fillet in the middle of a piece of cling film, measuring 36 x 30cm (14 x 10 inches). Mix together all the ingredients for the marinade, pour over the meat and spread evenly. Fold the cling film over the meat to hold the marinade next to it and seal. Leave to marinate for at least 1³/₄ hours. Remove the cling film, leaving the marinade attached to the meat. Cook the boar in a preheated oven at 220°C (425°F) mark 7 for 30-35 minutes.

Meanwhile, prepare the sauce. Put the demi glace into a saucepan and reduce by half. Add the prune juice and brandy. The sauce should be thick enough to coat the back of a spoon; if not reduce gently. Add the prunes to warm through. Just before serving, add a knob of butter.

Remove the boar from the oven and leave to rest in a warm place for a few minutes, then carve into thin slices. Arrange overlapping on warmed plates and pour over the sauce.

STEAMED BABY CARROTS

12 baby carrots, with leaves
salt

Clean the baby carrots, leaving a short green stub attached. Steam over boiling salted water for 3-5 minutes depending on their size.

ROAST PARSNIPS AND POTATOES

2 parsnips
2 large potatoes
olive oil for cooking
salt and freshly ground pepper

Cut the parsnips and potatoes into 2.5cm (1 inch) balls, using a melon baller. Place in a hot roasting tin, containing a little olive oil. Roast in a preheated oven at 200°C (400°F) mark 6 for 30 minutes. Season with salt and pepper to taste.

ROAST CHESTNUTS

I use the shelled pre-cooked chestnuts, which you can buy from delicatessens. They have no preservatives, last for ages and you can get them all year round.

12 chestnuts
melted butter for brushing

Brush the chestnuts with melted butter, then place in a preheated oven at about 170°C (325°F) mark 3 for 10 minutes, just to warm through.

To serve, imagine each serving plate as a triangle. At one point, place a tiny bunch of carrots; at another the potatoes and parsnips; at the other point, place the 3 chestnuts. Serve immediately.

PEAR GRATIN WITH CINNAMON ICE CREAM

Ice Cream:
300ml (1/2 pint) milk
300ml (1/2 pint) cream
1 cinnamon stick
4 egg yolks
125g (4 oz) sugar

Gratin:
4 ripe pears
lemon juice for sprinkling
4 egg yolks
45ml (3 tbsp) caster sugar
100ml (3 1/2 fl oz) double cream, whipped
125ml (4 fl oz) Poire William eau-de-vie

To make the ice cream, put the milk and cream in a saucepan with the cinnamon stick and heat gently. Simmer for 5 minutes to infuse. Remove from the heat.

Beat the egg yolks and sugar together thoroughly to a creamy consistency, then whisk into the milk. Remove the cinnamon stick, squeezing all the juice from the stick into the mixture. Transfer to a freezerproof container and freeze for approximately 2 hours, or until it is the consistency of ice cream.

For the gratin, peel, core and slice the pears, then sprinkle with lemon juice to prevent browning. Arrange in 4 small gratin dishes or on heatproof plates. Beat the egg yolks and sugar together thoroughly, then fold in the whipped cream and Poire William. Pour the mixture over the pears, coating them completely. Bake in a preheated oven at 220°C (425°F) mark 7 for 10-15 minutes. Allow to stand for 5 minutes before serving.

Just before serving, place a scoop of cinnamon ice cream in the centre of each pear gratin. Serve immediately.

INDEX

OF RECIPE TITLES AND CONTESTANTS